Don't Tell Me I Can't

Don't Tell Me I Can't

IT'S NEVER TOO LATE

Mary Jane Robinson

ISBN-13: 9781530707775
ISBN-10: 1530707773

Dedication

I would like to dedicate this book to my mother, Amelia Marie Vecca. My mother was taken home to be with the Lord at the age of 65 after many years of battling emphysema. She was 100 percent devoted to being a full time wife and mother. She was a strong Catholic and an avid reader. She was the most selfless person that I have ever met in my entire life. She never got her high school diploma and never got her driver's license. She taught me to stand up for myself and not to ever compare myself with anyone else. She also was the most trustworthy and truthful person I had in my life. I could tell her anything and everything, and she would not blink an eye. If I asked for her opinion, she would give me the truth, not the answer that I wanted to hear. My only regret is that she will never get to read my book, because she has been the biggest inspiration to get me where I am today.

Preface

I AM WRITING THIS BOOK for all those who doubt their ability to reach their goals in life. You first have to make the decision to push forward no matter what your obstacles are, and to put your faith in God that He will see you through to the end.

I believe God has given me the gift of encouragement. It has been on my heart to encourage those I meet, especially the younger generation. I want to encourage them that they can be anything that they dream to be, and to build up their self-esteem and self-worth. So many young people of this generation are left to themselves, with no one there to encourage them or give them the love they need. No matter where I go, there is always someone I can speak to or smile at in an effort to build them up. I believe that is the very least that we Christians can do in our lifetime.

Before I became a Christian, I went to church, but I didn't really know God. I didn't acknowledge that Jesus Christ died for my sins. I went to church out of habit or ritual. I did not have the realization that God is my Father, that He loves me more than my earthly parents could ever love me. As a Christian it is a comfort and a blessing to know that God is our heavenly Father, that we are His children, that we are heirs to His riches and glory. To have that peace in knowing that God the creator of the universe loves me and is with me get me through even the toughest times in my life. I truly believe what God's word tells us in Mathew 19:26 "All things are possible with God", and I pray that after you read this book and see how God did the impossible in my life, you will believe it too.

CHAPTER 1

I WAS BORN ON APRIL 28, 1958, the fifth of seven children of Sebastian and Amelia Vecca. (Newt and Mel for short) I was told that when my mother was pregnant with me, her doctor told her in her fifth month that she would be delivering a still born baby, because they could not detect a heartbeat. (Ultrasound did not exist back then) My mom told me that she would rub her tummy to try to get me to move, but I never did. Long story short, when my mom went into labor she and dad were shocked that I was alive and healthy. Since my parents were not expecting to deliver a healthy baby, they never picked out a name, even though they did pick out who my god parents would be. My god parents had a daughter, Mary Jane, so that is who I am named after. For many years, I wondered what happened while I was in my mother's womb. Now that I am a Christian, I truly believe that satan was trying to destroy me way back then because God had a plan for my life.

Growing up in a strict Italian/Catholic family was typical in my neighborhood. We were fortunate enough to have been born during a time when there was nothing to do inside the house, and so everyone was forced to go outside and play. We all walked to the same bus stop every morning, planning what we were going to do when we got out of school. Almost everyone in our neighborhood went to the same elementary school and high school, and back then, believe it or not, we had kids who walked to school every day, if they lived close enough to the school. Most of us also went to the same church and went to Sunday school together, as well. So when you grew up in a neighborhood, you basically spent your entire childhood with the same group of friends. Since most of the kids my age were boys, I grew up a tom boy. We played baseball, made forts, played kick the can, went sled riding, ice skating, kick ball you name it. I learned very early on how to defend myself and defend my brothers and sisters. I never took any crap from anyone then and still don't to this day. Did I mention that I was 5 feet tall and 100 pounds back then?

Most of my fond childhood memories are of all good times we had in our neighborhood. We basically just went home to eat, use the bathroom (if we were not in the woods) and sleep. My father worked two jobs as far back as I can remember, and my mom was a stay home mom, who never even got her driver's license. I had three older brothers, Carl, Danny and Mike, an older sister, Phyllis, a younger sister, Janice, and a younger brother, Jimmy. The one strong common bond amongst all of my siblings was that we all had a great sense of humor and loved busting on each other. There was a big age gap between the three older boys and the rest of us and they definitely did their share of bossing us around. When dad wasn't home, which was quite often because he worked two jobs to support our family, my older brothers took advantage of every opportunity they had to "take charge" of us girls and our younger brother. The boys had no problem taking the phone from us and hanging up on our friends when they needed to use it. We could be in the middle of a show or movie on TV and the boys would just come in and change the channel. Mom definitely took care of most of these situations, but sometimes she would just let us fight it out and she would go into her room and escape into one of her books. We didn't even think of squealing on the boys when dad got home, because the next time we would get it even worse for getting them in trouble. The one good thing that came out of all this battling, was that all three of us girls learned how to fight and defend ourselves.

When Dad was home, we had to be quiet. We always ate dinner together at 5:00 p.m., as soon as Dad got home from his day job. Dinner time was sometimes fun, but most of the time it was when Dad had our undivided attention, and he was giving out the orders for the week. After dinner, Dad would go from house to house repairing televisions sets. When he came home, he would go straight to bed and no one was allowed to make any noise (it was lights out at 9:00 p.m. during the week). This was always a problem, since there were eight other people living in a small six room cape with a bath and a half, who were still wide awake, just getting out of work, needing to shower, etc.

Dad was a control freak. He handled all the money, (what little we had) and mom had no say in anything. We probably would have been considered a "poor" family, but we never actually realized it. We lived on hand me downs from friends and relatives, or from each other. When one of us outgrew our clothes or a bike, it was handed down to the next one in line. From as far back as I can remember, I can hear my Dad complaining about how much money he had to spend on groceries, the light bill, the water bill or whatever. We all learned quickly how to take a very fast shower and to make sure we turned lights off as soon as we left a room. Dad was tough on my older brothers because they were given the responsibility of mowing the lawn, taking out the garbage and driving my mom to the grocery store or one of us to a doctor's appointment. When dad wasn't around, there were the constant arguments between my older brothers about who did what last and who was too busy to give one of us a ride.

As for us girls, well we had to do all the household chores. We were never allowed outside until our chores were done, and forget about even thinking about getting an allowance! We were lucky enough to be living at home for free. If we wanted anything we had to find odd jobs to do to make money. My brothers had paper routes and shoveled snow in the winter. I began baby-sitting for the next door neighbor when I was 12. Dad only shelled out his cash for my two sisters, whom he favored, because they were the only ones he showed love and affection to. Our younger brother was the baby in the family, and he was spoiled by all of us.

For some reason, my dad felt the need to constantly point about how stubborn I was and to complain about how difficult I was. (I look back and thank God that I was a strong willed child) My father was never wrong, and if you disagreed with him, you had a serious problem. My worst childhood memories are the hurtful things my father said and did to me. My two sisters were his favorites. He even talked to me in a harsh tone, which made me nervous to speak to him because I didn't want him to snap at me. He would constantly grab my sisters and say in front of me, "these are my two beautiful girls". He was always making sure he commented on my frizzy hair, my mustache (yes, I am Italian) my acne, my big nose, my hairy arms or my wide feet. He would get mad if I wasn't smiling when I got home and would start harassing me, asking me "what's the matter now" "you're never happy you miserable little bitch" or if it was a bad acne day "what's the matter Scarface?". It seems that he got some sort of pleasure putting me down and pointing out my flaws. He would point out my flaws every chance he had, for whatever reason, especially in front of my older brothers. So I guess this made it okay for my brothers to repeat some of dad's degrading remarks whenever they felt like it, even in front of him.

Needless to say, I hated my Dad because he favored my two sisters and was cruel to me. In my mind I knew that I would never be as pretty as my sisters, and I was frustrated because there was nothing I could do to change that. Not only were his degrading remarks hurtful, my dad would never tell me that he loved me. I heard him say it to my sisters and younger brother, but never to me. Fortunately, I was a straight A student, which they weren't, so I worked even harder at school, hoping Dad would notice that. The only recognition I received was Dad saying "well at least she got my brain". Dad was smart, but that comment never seemed to come across as a compliment. As I got into my teenage years, the critical comments about my appearance killed my self-esteem. I resolved to myself that I couldn't do anything about my looks or my hair, but I could exercise and make sure that my body was in the best shape it could be in. When I got my first full time job, it started electrolysis treatments to get rid my mustache and hairy arms, in an attempt to feel better about my appearance. Even when I did get compliments about my appearance, I thought others just said that to make me feel better about myself.

Thank God my mother and I had a very close relationship. She would encourage me as best she could and tried to explain to me that my dad really didn't mean what he said. It didn't matter, how much she tried to convince me, I knew Dad never loved me and no matter how hard I tried, I could never seem to please him. Dad's favoritism of my sisters over me also killed any relationship I tried to have with my sisters, because whenever we would argue amongst ourselves, I was always the one that was wrong or the trouble maker.

Sad to say that at that time, I hated my sisters because they knew just how to work dad to get him to believe them and to get dad to give them anything they wanted. On the up side, this also made me very independent, because I would never ask my father for anything, to prove the point that I didn't need him. For many years I went through very long periods of time not speaking one word to my dad, unless I had to give an answer for something. Whenever I was in a real bind and did need to ask dad for money, he would either say he didn't have any or he would take out his wallet and throw the money at me. Most of the time it wasn't what my dad actually said or did to me, it was the hurtful tone of voice that he would use whenever I would speak to him. He always talked to me like I was a stupid piece of garbage, in a rude condescending way. To this day, if anyone talks to me in that tone of voice, my defenses and walls go right up. If I didn't want to share my clothes or makeup with my sisters, and dad would hear us arguing, he would come right up and start yelling at me and calling me a dirty, rotten skunk or selfish bitch.

I went to high school from 1972 to 1976. By this time, dad was doing better financially and he was able to send my younger sister and brother to a Catholic grammar school. My dad had me take the entrance exam for one of the Catholic high schools, which I passed with a very high score. However, all of my friends were going to the public high school, and I wanted to stay with my friends. Dad wasn't happy about my decision, and to be honest, I cannot remember how I ever got my way. By this time, I was the fifth "Vecca" child to go to the public high school in our district. The principal and vice principal were very familiar with my older siblings, and I heard all the stories of the trouble they got into. My first day of high school as a freshman was one I will never forget. My sister, Phyllis, and her friends brought me to school that day and showed me around before classes started. My sister and her friends decided to use the girl's room before the bell rang, so I went too. Well, they decided to smoke a joint in the girl's room, and as luck would have it, a teacher came in and caught them, and dragged all of us down to the principal's office. I hadn't even made it to my first class yet! My sister was starting her senior year, and the principal was already ready to suspend her. Somehow, we all caught a break, but I was scared out of my wits!

My best friend in high school was Kenda, whom I also went to grammar school with. Kenda came from a well to do family, and before she was 16, there was a brand new, bright and shiny, yellow Firebird in her driveway with a license plate with her name on it, waiting for her. Once, Kenda got her driver's license, we were off to the local plaza parking lot where everyone hung out. Kenda and I were never really attracted to any of the guys our age at school, we liked the older guys who hung out "down town". Both Kenda and I were straight "A" students, but we never joined any of the school clubs or attended many school athletic games. I did want to be a cheerleader, but I needed to find a job after school as soon as turned 16, so I couldn't join because practice was right after school. My first job was in a local market in the meat department. I resented the fact that I had to work every day after school, but if I wanted new clothes, money in my pocket and to try to save for a car, I had no other choice.

One of the most difficult times in my high school years was when a guy that I was seeing got killed in a motor vehicle accident in his senior year. Rocky (way before the Stallone movies) was a couple of years older than me, and was also from a wealthy family. Rocky was speeding one night, lost control of his car and crashed into a telephone pole. He died on the way to the hospital. I had never experienced anything that shocking and traumatic, and it took me a while to recover from that. Whenever I drove by the spot where the accident occurred, my heart would ache.

Back in the 70's the legal drinking age was 18, so Kenda and I were sneaking into bars when we were 16 and 17. Back then the first license that was issued was only a typed piece of paper. Kenda and I both changed our birth year from 1958 to 1956 on our licenses, and got in bars with no problems, usually. There was one time when a friend of my brother, Mike, was the bouncer at the door and he decided to hold my license up to the light and saw where I had changed the year. All he said was "nice try little Vecca, come back in a couple of years". We just laughed it off and went somewhere else. Oh well, those were the good old days! Once we graduated from high school, Kenda and I went our separate ways, but we rekindled our friendship many times over the years and continue to this day.

CHAPTER 2

By the age of 21, I moved out of the family home and into an apartment with my friend, Patti Layden. Patti and I met while working in a local department store. I started working there in my senior year of high school. When Patti and I first met, we did not like each other. However, one day in the break room we started talking about all the things we used to do to straighten our hair, and we hit it off from that day on. I soon found out that Patti also had abusive issues with her step dad, so we had something else in common. When Patti turned 18, her parents sent her off on her own, because they said that she was no longer their responsibility. Her mom and stepdad sold the family home and moved into an apartment, so Patti had no choice but to find somewhere else to live. Patti is four years older than me, and by the time I moved in with her, she had lived in five or six different places with other people. The apartment she was living in was in a low income area in town, on the second floor of a three family. No matter how bad it was, it still was 100 percent better than living home, but I did miss my mom a lot. But once I made the decision, there was no turning back. Despite how many times my Dad told me that I would never be able to make it out on my own, I thought to myself "Don't tell me I can't".

Shortly before moving out, I received my Associates Degree in Executive Secretarial Science at the local community college. Being a secretary was not my first choice of a career. I wanted to be an accountant, because I was very good at math. My dad convinced me that I was too nervous of a person to be an accountant. He'd say, "You think you have ulcers now, wait when tax time comes around each year, the pressure will be overwhelming". Well, since I had already experienced the pain of suffering with ulcers, I was "convinced" that I definitely was not the right type of person who could handle the pressures of being an accountant. My next choice was to be a teacher, which dad also convinced me was not a good idea, "because teachers don't make that much money, and all summer you have no income coming in". Since I was always trying to find ways to please my dad, I took his advice. Sadly, I didn't even discuss my career choices with my high school counselors or anyone else, because "dad was always right". It's difficult for me to look back and see what a hold my dad had on me. Even though I "hated" him for how he treated me, I was still always trying to find ways to get dad to love me. It wasn't until much later in my life, through counseling, that I learned I had suffered from verbal abuse from my father. I will delve into that further later on in this book.

Shortly after graduating, I landed a full time job in a local law firm as a legal secretary. Patti was working her way up in the retail business and started training for a management position. Our apartment was modest to say the least, a four room apartment on the second floor, across the street from a cemetery. Our standard joke was that most of the neighborhood was dead and the rest were raising hell. Anyway, it was nice to finally have my own room and my own bed. Growing up in our small six room cape, there was my parent's bedroom, the boys' room and the girls' room. I slept in a full size bed with my younger sister until I moved out. I was finally able to leave my makeup, toiletries and clothes out wherever I wanted, and they would still be where I left them when I came home.

I remember how good it felt to be out on my own, away from my father's hurtful comments. If I hadn't been a tomboy and made such great male friends, I don't think I would have ever let myself get close to any member of the opposite sex. If I had a bad day, I would always call my mom and she was always there to listen and give good honest advice. My parents' relationship had deteriorated about eight years before I moved out. My father would talk nasty to my mom and criticize her every chance he had. I would defend her whenever I witnessed him speaking to her like she was garbage. It wasn't until later in life that I realized that my mom and I were verbally abused. Verbal abuse was not even something that was recognized back then. There were no obvious scars or bruises, however, the pain is just as bad, if not worse than physical abuse. Everyone who met my dad thought he was the nicest, most generous, honest and caring man they have ever known. It would make me sick to my stomach to hear people tell me how "lucky" I was to have him as my father. Yes, my dad was a great provider for our family, working two jobs for years and a faithful church going man, but he had problems that were never addressed.

So here I was enjoying my single life and my friends, but there were days that I missed my sisters and brothers. I felt removed from them and their lives. My two oldest brothers were married before I moved out and had their own lives. I missed sitting at the kitchen table with my mom, pouring my heart out to her, and her listening endlessly. However, moving back was never an option for me because I would never let my father say that "he told me so".

After a year or so, I began to have this nagging empty feeling inside. I started to evaluate my life. The reality of being a "grown up" settled in. I started to feel like all there was to life was to work 9 to 5 for my paycheck to pay my bills, and to live it up on the weekend before starting all over on Monday. It seemed to me that this couldn't be all there was to life. I had a deep sense in my heart that there had to be a reason I was here, but I didn't exactly know what it was.

At about the same time, an old friend of Patti's invited her to her church one Sunday. Patti's friend was trying to get a basket of food by winning a challenge of bringing in the most visitors to her church. Patti asked me to come along to increase her friend's chance to win. I decided to go, but warned Patti and her friend that "no one better try to hug me or convert me". I remember the pastor was preaching that day of salvation and he asked for a raise of hands of all those who knew that if they would die today, that they would go to heaven. I was amazed at how many hands went up, as I was raised Catholic and believed that when we died we would go to purgatory until we were prayed out by our living relatives and friends here on earth. Let me stop right here. I know this may offend my Catholic brothers and sisters, but there is no mention in the Bible of purgatory. Believe me this stumbled me too, as I was raised with this belief all my life. But the fact remains, when we die we will be going to only one of two places, heaven or hell. The only way to heaven is through the blood of Jesus. He died on the cross to forgive all of our sins. All He asks is that we ask Him into our heart and live a life devoted to Him. It's that simple. Man just tries to complicate it because man is always looking for a way to compromise God's word. Trust me, there is such peace in knowing that you can have the promise of eternal life with God in this life. Wipe the dust off your Bible and see if what I am saying is true or not.

Anyway, I continued to listen to the pastor who said that all those who ask Jesus into their hearts would be given eternal life and be assured that they would go to be with the Lord when they died. At the end of the service, the pastor had an alter call and asked everyone to close their eyes and pray a simple prayer asking Jesus into their hearts. Well, I prayed that prayer that day and I became a born again Christian that Sunday in February of 1981. Patti also prayed the same prayer, but told me later that she had already asked Jesus into her heart months ago with her brother, Harry, who was an evangelist. The prayer of salvation is very simple and anyone can pray it at anytime and anywhere. A simple salvation prayer may go something like this:

Father, I know that I am a sinner and I know that your son, Jesus Christ, died on the cross for our sins. Father, I repent from my sins and I ask Jesus to come into my heart and forgive me of all my sins. Father I thank you for your promise of eternal life and I promise to live this day forward to please you. Amen.

Another gift I received after asking Jesus into my heart, was that His peace filled me. I was a worry wart since a very young girl. I used to worry about everything so bad that I developed ulcers by the age of 12. Most of my worries were that something would happen to our dad and we would not be able to support ourselves. Dad was famous for telling us that if he ever decided to leave or if he were to die, we would have nothing cause our mom never worked and "she never graduated from high school, so what job can she ever get". Welfare was not very big back in those days and I used to actually lay in bed at night and worry that we would all be orphans if something ever happened to dad. My other worries were that no one would ever like me because I was so ugly and so selfish. I worried that I would have to become a nun or something. I am not kidding you. I know this may sound foolish, but those were some of the worries that plagued my mind constantly as a young girl. God gave me the peace of mind that He will never leave me or forsake me, and I held on to that promise and His peace filled my soul.

Patti and I went to the Christian church we were saved in every Sunday, and began our Christian walk. That's when the trails came. The tenants on the first and third floors of our house were friends and they made more noise and caused more trouble than ever before. Being Christians, we tried our best to be Godly neighbors, but WHAT a test of our faith. However, no matter how awful the other tenants were, it was still better than living at home. I loved my independence and learned early on how to depend on God for all my needs, and how to love the unlovely.

Patti and I grew more like sisters. We had each other's backs and helped each other through the early years of our Christian walk. We got very involved in our church, and our church family came to mean more to both of us than our own families. The unconditional love was what drew us to our church family. The genuine thoughtfulness and unconditional love we received from our new brothers and sisters was something neither of us ever really experienced.

Patti and I also had the benefit of "knowing each other when". We went from working all week and getting high or drunk every weekend and chasing guys, to living a Christian lifestyle. It didn't happen that cut and dry though. We stopped going to bars because we had that keen sense of awareness that Jesus was with us everywhere we went, and we didn't want to bring him into bars. We did, however, still continue to smoke pot and did not get convicted of that for some time later. {that would be when we had a group of Christian friends over the apartment one day, and one of the guys found our stash and flushed it down the toilet}

My parents did not understand the new me. My father was upset that I "left the Catholic church" but my mother knew me well enough that I would not just follow some cult, and she actually noticed that I had changed for the better. In my heart I was disappointed that my dad was not happy that I became a Christian, but I had to put my feelings aside. I also had to tell my mother that we could not do anymore psychic readings, séances or palm readings. See my mom and I were heavy into psychic readings and she and my aunt told me that God had given me "a special gift", which they helped me develop. We were heavy into the psychic realm for at least seven or eight years, never knowing that God was against such things. When I got saved, my Christian brothers and sisters showed me many scriptures in the Bible that prohibited soothsaying or fortune telling. (See Exodus 7:11 and 22:18, Isaiah 47:9, Daniel 2:27, Numbers 22:7 and Jeremiah 10:2) It was very hard for me to accept it at first, because I was a good Catholic girl and would never do anything against our Lord. However, the more I studied the Bible, the more I realized that it was true, and I needed to tell my mom that she could not continue to do this because it opens the door for the devil to come into our lives. I know that may sound hokey, but it is true. Whenever you open up yourself to the spiritual world, you open yourself up to all spirits good and evil. Thank God I was protected all those years from any demon spirits entering into me. Mom was not receptive of what I had to tell her about the physic readings, but after I gave her all the Bible scriptures that I read, she realized it was true and we both promised each other and God that we would not continue this anymore, and we asked God to forgive us.

However, my friends would call me now and then to ask me what I "saw" about this or that and I would then explain that I did not do readings anymore and was able to give my testimony as to why. So God used that for His good in the end. Needless to say, many of my old friends did not like the "new" me because I wasn't the same anymore and we didn't have much in common anymore. When you give your heart to God and ask Him to come in and live in you, your life is going to change and those who you used to hang out with will no longer want to hang out with you anymore. Patti and I both experienced this in our lives at the same time, but we gained more Christian friends than the friends we lost. When I became a Christian, I soon realized who my real friends were because my real friends still accepted me, even if we didn't agree on everything. That is a true friend, one with whom you can be yourself with and they can do the same.

I would love to say that life was perfect from then on, but then I would be lying. I was a neat freak and Patti, was not. We were the female version of the Odd Couple in some ways. However, this really didn't cause much dissension between us. Neither of us were making much money back then and we had our share of financial problems. Most of our problems came from the junks that we drove. For example, in one of my cars the heater coil went, and all winter long I had to wrap a blanket around myself whenever I went anywhere. Patti had one car that had a passenger door that would not stay shut, so she had to tie the door to the steering wheel with a rope. One night, my sister, Phyllis, came out with us and we were all in the front seat. We forgot to tie the door and my sister almost fell out of the car when we went around a corner! We still laugh about that now and it's been over 30 years. In one year, I think we put the mechanic's son through a year of college. Sometimes our faith would be tested because we would wonder why things always had to be so difficult. We can look back now and realize it was during those times that our faith was made strong, because God was always faithful and we never were late in paying any of our bills.

As time went on, Patti and I became more and more involved in our church. We both felt that we had a reason to be here on this earth, although we weren't exactly sure of what our callings were. When things at our apartment finally got unbearable, we moved in to a new apartment in a much nicer neighborhood. It was a two family home and the landlords, an Italian couple with a daughter about our age, lived on the first floor. The rent was very affordable for us and we had off street parking! No more having to leave half of our furniture in the street to save the parking spot that we had shoveled out. Unless you have ever experienced this, you will never know how awful parking on a city street in the winter can be. As Christians we tried to "turn the other cheek" as the Bible tells us, but trust me, sometimes we definitely struggled with this when we would get home and would have to park half way down the street from our apartment.

Our new apartment was truly a blessing because we finally were able to have people over, and not have to worry about our neighbors fighting or playing their music loud. It was almost like living "with" a family. Our landlady loved to bake, and she would always send us up desserts and cookies that she made. Patti and I became very friendly with our landlords' daughter, and many times we were able to share the Lord with her. Our next door neighbor was a nice older man and his wife, who always gave us fresh food from his garden. The landlord would clear the driveway in the winter for us (if we gave him some money for gas for his snow blower), but it was still better than having to shovel it ourselves! Our rent was very affordable, and the landlord never raised the rent for the entire time we lived there. God was again faithful to answer our prayers and bless us. Patti and I even went to the local Toyota dealership and ordered two brand new Toyota Corollas. It was one of those push, pull or drag deals and we literally did just that with our trade-ins! Patti and I were grateful for what God was doing in our lives and our finances.

CHAPTER 3

I SPENT MY EARLY AND mid-twenties living the Christian life, working in the law firm and attending church services. Dating was not a big part of my life or Patti's. We made up our minds that we were only going to date Christian guys, so that definitely limited the selection. However, our well-meaning friends and relatives continued to bombard us with "I have this real nice guy I want you to meet". When I would ask if the guy was a Christian, I would get the answer, "Yes he goes to church". (Unfortunately going to church doesn't make you a Christian any more than going to McDonalds makes you a hamburger) What I was looking for was a man who loved God like I did, read the bible, and lived a life that honored God. I would decline the offers and many of my friends, family and co-workers "worried" that I was going to be an old maid because I was waiting for someone that didn't exist. Trust me there were days that I worried about that myself, but I knew in my heart that my life was in God's hands and He would give me the desires of my heart in His time. By this time I had been a bridesmaid in many weddings and deep in my heart I did desire to have a husband and family, but I did not want to settle for second best, just because I was too impatient to wait on God for His best for me.

My life was full, I was a Youth Group Leader in my church, I enjoyed my nieces and nephews and I was happy. Funny when you are happy, people just have to make sure that they point out the one or two areas of your life that they feel are lacking. Thank God He always gave me the grace to get through the holidays, as those were the most difficult times, as a single woman. It was especially hard at the holidays because that is when those well-meaning relatives would make sure to tell me that I was "getting near the end of the child bearing age". Okay, thank you for your thoughtfulness and concern, and your ignorance for making such a stupid comment! Sometimes I marvel at things that people say.

Not only was I in my late twenties and not married, I was still a virgin. If people weren't wondering how I could still be a virgin, they were wondering what was wrong with me. The honest trust is that having lots of guy friends from early on in my life, I had always felt more comfortable around guys than I did around girls. So, over the years I had more male friends than female friends. When I would hang out with my guy friends, I would hear them talk about their girlfriends behind their backs. The guys couldn't wait to tell each other when they FINALLY got in so and so's pants and how she looked with her clothes off, ect. I would be amazed how my guy friends would talk when their girlfriends weren't around. I learned that with guys it was all about when they were going to get a girl to give in, and all the crap that they will say and do just to accomplish that. I thought to myself that I was never going to give any guy the opportunity to talk about me that way. So, that was one reason I chose not to have sex. The other reason was that because I believed that I wasn't that pretty, but had a cute shape, I just figured that if any guy was going to go out with me that they really just wanted one thing, and they weren't getting it from me! I am not trying to say that I never had a boyfriend or went on dates, because I did, but when the guy was starting to make sex an issue or topic in our relationship, I was no longer interested. When I became a Christian, then I didn't have sex for the main reason that the Bible forbids sex outside of marriage, and I didn't want to displease God.

Now if you are reading this and you are not a virgin, the good news is that if you repent (stop having sex) and ask God to forgive you, you are a new creature and all your former sins will be wiped away and you will become a new person. It is as if God gives you a brand new start on life, with a clean slate, so you can renew yourself and be a virgin in God's eyes and in your heart. It says in 2 Corinthians 5:17 "Therefore, if anyone is in Christ, he is a new creation, behold the old is gone and the new one has begun".

A year or so after I moved out on my own, my relationship with my sisters began to improve. My sisters would call and visit me quite often, and we would talk about a lot of things that went on at home with dad. My sisters each had serious co-dependency issues from being so controlled and influenced by our dad. Dad had even tried to get my sisters to turn against our mom, when he and my mom began having their marriage problems. However, when my sisters and I were teenagers, mom was diagnosed with emphysema, from years of smoking, and not long after, needed to be hooked up to an oxygen tank 24/7. Mom's illness and her unbelievable loyalty to her wifely duties, gave us all even more respect and love for her. There was no way any of us would do anything to hurt our mom.

My mom lived a very simple life. She gave everything for her family. She never asked for anything for herself. Her entire wardrobe could fit in one large garbage bag. She kept up with loads and loads of laundry, put a hot meal on the table every evening and waited up for each of us to get home safely every night. When my parents' relationship began to fall apart, she never stopped doing everything. By this time, we were all telling mom to leave dad, but she wouldn't hear of it. She took her vows seriously, and never tried to turn us against our dad. We all went out of our way to make sure that mom had what she needed, and get her to her doctor's appointments. In a way, mom's illness drew all of us closer to her and closer to each other. She was the rock in the family, and at least one of us would talk to her every day to make sure she was okay.

During the years after moving out on my own, my two sisters and my three older brothers got married, and had children. My older sister, Phyllis, had moved to Texas for a while to stay with a high school friend whose husband was stationed in an Army base there, and shortly after arriving in Texas, she met and eventually married an Army buddy of her friends' husband. My sister moved from Texas to Louisiana before settling in Nebraska, where her husband was from. The rest of my brothers and my younger sister still lived in town, so we kept in touch.

As time went on, mom's illness worsened and she had developed congestive heart failure. Mom was hospitalized numerous times throughout the years because she would be struggling to breathe. It was during those times my dad would tell me how God always keeps one child single to take care of their parents, and I was that child. I remember telling my dad that I was praying to be married someday, and he would tell me that God's plan was for me to move back home and help him take care of my mother. I was still so influenced by my dad that I needed to go for counseling with my pastor. My pastor told me that my dad was just being selfish, and told me to continue to believe God for a husband. So, that's exactly what I did, I continued to pray and believe God that he heard my prayers and would answer them in His time.

I want to mention to those reading this whose parent or parents are not treating them properly or providing for them that it is not your fault that you are being treated that way. Just because people become parents, they don't automatically become good moms and dads. I never had the dad I always wished I had. I know that it is very hard to understand how a parent can be so cruel and mean to their own children, but it is them that have a problem. I had to come to the point where I had to accept that I was not going to have a father who loved and cared for me. That I wasn't going to have the dad like other people had. Be encouraged, God is our Heavenly Father and He loves us. He wants the best for us and will never leave or forsake us. Please take comfort in that and believe that He has a good plan for your life.

CHAPTER 4

In 1987, Patti got involved in a Singles Group at a local Christian church and met a nice Christian guy. I didn't attend because I was busy with our Youth Group. One of the girls at our church started to teach me how to play simple cords on the guitar. I wanted to try to learn how to play for our Youth Group, so I could lead them in song when we got together. I remember thinking and praying about attending the Singles Group, because after all, how was I going to meet anyone if I spent my spare time with teenagers? I distinctly remember being in church one Sunday and God spoke to my heart and asked me, "Would you still serve me and love me even if I never give you a husband? Would you serve me for nothing in return?" I remember sitting there with a pain in my heart, knowing how much I loved God, but still questioning myself. It was then and there that I decided that I needed to stop praying and asking God for a husband and family and simply live each day for God as best I could and trust Him for His best for my life. It was a big relief for me to stop trying to figure it all out and to trust God that he heard my prayers and believe that he would answer in His time.

In 1988, my younger brother, Jimmy, got engaged and was planning to get married in September of 1989. I remember my mom telling me that she did not want to die before all her children were settled down, and she said she was praying that I would marry before she died. Mom knew my hearts' desire, and she also knew I was trusting God with this. In early 1989, my mom got very ill, and we almost lost her. She was no longer able to make dinner, do the laundry, she needed help to bathe and use the toilet. My dad knew that he was going to be alone with mom and he would have to be her caretaker, he did not want to do that. During of my mom's hospitalizations, I was at my parents' home to get some of her things and my dad was there. He was in a very bad mood because the doctor told him that he would have to hire visiting nurses to take care of my mother or he would have to take care of her himself. I remember standing in their kitchen and he stopped me on my way out and told me that I needed to quit my job, move back home and take care of my mother. When I told him, that no matter how much I loved my mother, I was not going to move home. My dad became furious and began calling me every nasty and hurtful name that he could think of. This time, however, I stood up to him and told him that I was no longer a little girl, and he could not talk to me that way anymore. He threw me out of his house and told me I was never any good anyway.

I remember driving away, crying hysterically, barely able to see through my tears. I knew how much I loved my mom, but I could never move back into that house with him. I prayed for a miracle for my mom, I asked God to heal her so she would not have to depend on my father for her care. I was so upset at the whole situation, my heart was torn, and I hated my dad for putting me in that position in the first place. I was also sad for my mom because now she had to really depend on him.

Well, thank God mom returned home better than expected, and we found out that the visiting nurses care would be covered by dad's insurance, so she would be taken care of. My brother's wedding was seven months away, and mom was going to be well enough to attend. I took mom to get a dress for the wedding, and she was happy that she was feeling better.

On July 4, 1989, Patti and I went to our church picnic. The picnic was attended by parishioners of our church and two other churches that our congregation was affiliated with. We had attended many church picnics in the past, not to mention numerous dinners, baptisms and functions that our churches had over the years. We always loved these gatherings because we would see different sisters and brothers that lived in different parts of the State, and we would also have a chance to see if there were any eligible bachelors! Well, we didn't scope out anyone special at the Fourth of July picnic, but we had a good time as usual.

However, a couple of weeks later, my pastor came up to me and told me that a guy, Jim, from our Willimantic church saw me at the picnic and asked him if I was seeing anyone. My pastor told the guy that as far as he knew I wasn't, and the guy asked my pastor for my phone number. My pastor was now asking me if I would like Jim to give me a call. I was very hesitant because Willimantic was 90 miles away from Waterbury. My first question to my pastor was, "What's wrong with this guy that he wants to drive 90 miles for a date with me?" My pastor just laughed and said, "Nothing, just talk to him when he calls, and if you feel right about it, then see what happens".

Well, my brother's wedding was coming up in a couple of months and we had a bridal shower for my future sister-in-law to plan, not to mention that I spent my spare time visiting my mom. There were no cell phones at the time, so every time Jim tried to call me, I wasn't home. Finally, on a Sunday night in early August, Jim called and I was home.

Jim and I talked on the phone for over an hour. He was very sweet and said that he had been praying and asking God for a Christian girl, and when he saw me at the picnic he felt that God had shown him that "I was the one". Well, you can imagine my reaction! Are you serious right now?? Great now this crazy guy has my number! But, Jim kept calling and we both found out that we were supporting a child in Haiti at the same mission. We both had moved out on our own at an early age. Jim was 30 and I was 31, and we both were at the time in our lives where we felt that we wanted to be married and have a family. We seemed to be hitting it off on the phone, but deep inside I couldn't help but think that this guy must have something wrong with him. Patti and I asked around about Jim, none of the people we knew seemed to know who he was or even what he looked like. I remember telling Patti that he must be creepy looking or something because we certainly would have noticed him at the picnic if he wasn't. None the less, the more we talked on the phone, the more I was growing to like this "mystery" man. I started thinking how shallow would I be if when Jim and I finally did meet, I didn't like his appearance. I was nervous about having to hurt his feelings.

During the time Jim and I spent talking on the phone, I didn't tell my family or co-workers about him, just in case nothing came about between us.

One day Jim sent flowers to my job, and I met the delivery man at the elevator, and grabbed the card out fast. I blew it off by saying that the flowers were from a client to show their appreciation. Well the girls bought it, but a week later another bouquet arrived at the office. This time the girls marched the flowers over to my desk, and demanded that I open the card in front of them. Well, my secret was out, but I honestly didn't know where this relationship was going. I told them the whole story and they were teasing me saying "your Prince Charming has arrived". I assured them that they will be the first to know when Jim and I finally get together. I had been working with my co-workers for over eight years at the time, and they knew how I felt about dating. They were excited for me and were convinced that Jim must be the person that I had been praying for.

Well, our schedules finally coincided, and Jim and I scheduled our first date for Saturday, September 1st. We decided that Jim would drive down to Waterbury and then we would go to the Bethlehem Fair. I remember Patti and I waiting in our kitchen, looking out the window, for Jim to arrive. When his car finally pulled in, I told Patti to "check him out first" because I was too nervous. Patti looks out the window as Jim is getting out of his car, careful to hide behind the curtain, and tells me he has a bouquet of flowers in his hands. I'm like yeah, yeah, how does he look???? Patti says, "Mar he looks handsome from here." Next thing we know, Jim is at the door, and the moment we've been waiting for is here. To my surprise, I was pleasantly greeted by this tall, handsome guy with these big dark brown eyes and awesome smile! Patti and I caught each other's eye and she mouths "holy crap" to me! I invited Jim to come in and tell him how nice it was to finally meet him after all those hours talking on the phone. Patti went to grab a vase for the flowers, and then excuses herself. So here we are face to face and now neither one of us can think of anything to say. Thank God, Patti came back into the kitchen and started up a conversation and broke the ice for us.

After a few minutes, we left and headed for the fair. I kept thinking to myself, there just has to be something wrong with this guy. Because of my low self-esteem, I couldn't help but keep thinking that a guy this handsome, sweat, God fearing guy can't possibly have to look 90 miles away from his home for a girlfriend. I was expecting Jim to be just this average looking guy, maybe losing his hair, overweight or something, but here he was this tall, dark and handsome guy, great head of hair, beautiful straight teeth and an awesome body! So we spend a beautiful fall day at the fair and at the end of our first date, Jim gives me a kiss on the cheek and asks me if he can call me again. I'm thinking to myself "are you kidding me?", and I tell him that I had a great day and I definitely wanted him to call me again.

After Jim left, I jumped on the phone to call my mom and my sisters, who were just as anxious as I was for the "big day". Well, now my mom says that Jim has to come to Sunday dinner and so she and my family can meet him. At the time Jim was living his grandmother at her house on a lake. Jim was not used to Italians like us, and I was nervous because I figured well, this will be the ultimate test. If Jim can handle all of us on a Sunday afternoon at my parents' home for our weekly pasta dinner, then he must be okay. Also, I had a very close relationship with my mother, and I wanted her to meet Jim, and give me her approval, before I would let our relationship go any further. I trusted and valued my mom's opinion so much that if she would have told me that she did not feel that Jim was good for me, I honestly would have ended our relationship, or at least would not have let it get serious.

Over the years when I was growing up, my mom was the only person who would give me her honest opinion, even when it was not the answer that she knew I wanted to hear. I remember so many times my mom would tell me, if a guy likes you, he will call you. When I was still living home and dates would come to pick me up, she would definitely tell me if she liked or disliked the guy, and 90 percent of the time she was right on. Mom would never tell you what you wanted to hear, unless it was actually the truth. That was one of the special qualities that I loved about my mom. She was usually always right about our friends and our dates. Mom just had that gift of discernment and she was not afraid to share it with her children.

So, the following Sunday after our first date, Jim came down early and went to church with Patti and I and then we headed up to my parents' house. I can't remember if all of my brothers and their wives were there that Sunday, but I do remember the house was full as usual. By this time, I had about six nieces and nephews, so our family was big. Jim just had one sister, so he was not used to such a large family together all at once. The moment came and we arrived at my parents' house, and there was a line of cars in the street in front of the house. Jim was like, "do all these cars belong to your family"? Yep! We go in and mom's busy in the kitchen getting things ready and my sister, Janice, meets us at the door. I introduce Jim to everyone and we sit down to eat. Mom and dad ask the usual questions about what kind of job he had and how much money he had in the bank! Just kidding, but they did seem to like Jim, and I was relieved, but I still needed to get mom's opinion.

After Jim and I left and he drove me home, I asked him what he thought of my family. Jim said he thought we were all loud and crazy, but he assured me that he enjoyed himself and was very happy that he met them. We said our good-byes at my apartment, and made our next date for the following week-end for me to come and meet his family. Right after Jim left, I called mom and asked her "Well???" My mom was happy to tell me that she thought Jim was a very nice guy and she thought he was very sincere. She then went on to tell me that she thought he was "the one". Well, now I had mom's approval, so the rest was up to God's will for my life.

Now the next step was for me to meet Jim's family. Jim's parents were divorced when he and his sister were very young. Jim and his sister, Rhonda, lived with their mom. Jim's dad remarried and had two more children. By the time Jim's step brother and sister came along, Jim's dad had moved up in the company he was working in and was very successful. Jim's stepbrother and stepsister lived a very different life style than he and his sister did. Anyway, at the time, Jim's mother had remarried a very nice man named, Eddie. Jim's dad was divorced from his second wife, and was engaged to be married to his third wife. So my meeting Jim's family had to come in steps. Therefore, we planned that the following weekend I would drive up to his part of the State and stay overnight at his grandmother's house on Saturday night, go to Jim's church in the morning and then his mom's for lunch.

Since Jim lived in the country, off the main highways, he met me on an exit and I followed him to his grandmother's house. When I FINALLY got there, I remember that I kept thinking how our relationship was ever going to actually work with such a far distance between us. Anyways, we pulled into the driveway. It was a beautiful Fall afternoon and the sun was shining over the lake at his grandmother's house. When we came into the house the very first thing that his grandmother said to me was, "Well so this is the girl that my grandson is racking up $200.00 phone bills with". Wow, what was I supposed to say? I just looked at Jim and said, "Yep, that's me". Talk about breaking the ice! I wasn't sure how to take that remark, so I just let it go. From there it was the usual questions, where I lived, where I worked, etc. We had a cup of coffee and chatted for a bit longer, and then Jim and I went out to dinner.

The next morning we went to church and it was really nice to see our Christian brothers and sisters and we were blessed with many wishes of God's best for us. After church we headed for Jim's mom's house. When we arrived Jim's mom and her husband were very friendly and made me feel welcome and comfortable. I remember driving home that afternoon and talking to God and praying that He would show Jim and I His will for our lives and show us how to continue in our relationship.

CHAPTER 5

My brother, Jimmy's, wedding was at the end of September. Jim couldn't make it to the wedding and Patti and I went together. My sisters couldn't wait to let all my relatives know that I had met a guy, and that he was possibly "the one". My aunts, uncles and cousins were all happy for me and said they couldn't wait to meet Jim.

Jim and I continued to date on the weekends and talk on the phone during the week. By now we had fallen in love with each other and we actually talking about a future together. On November 11th, we both had the day off and Jim asked me if I wanted to go to the beach. We both loved the beach, and we would go there sometimes and take walks. We get to the beach and we are walking along the sandbar and Jim stops by a rock edge and we sit down with our feet in the water, enjoying a beautiful fall day. All of the sudden, Jim gets up and kneels down in front of me, takes a little box out of his pocket, opens it up and asked me to marry him. Well, of course I said YES! Not only did Jim ask me to marry him, he had a specific date in mind, April 21, 1990. He also had a brochure to go on a on our honeymoon on a Christian cruise that was set to sail out of Florida the next day. I was completely taken back with everything, and I said that I needed to check with my parents. Jim then assured me that they would be okay with it because he went to my parents' house first and asked my dad for his permission to marry me.

Well, April was only six months away. The girls at the office were happy for me, but were uneasy with how fast our relationship was going. The only answer I had was that God had brought us together, we were sure of that and we were 30 years old and there really wasn't any reason to wait.

So the wedding plans began. The first things we had to take care of were the church and the reception hall, and as the Lord would have it, both had the date open, so the date was booked. I asked Patti to be my maid of honor and my sister, Janice, to be my matron of honor, and they agreed. I then asked my two good friends, Patti and Kim, to be my bridesmaids, and they agreed.

A week later, Patti, Janice and myself went to the local bridal shop to pick out my gown and the bridesmaids gowns. I remember telling the woman who owned the shop that my fiancé and I were paying for our own wedding, and that I had budgeted $500.00 for my wedding gown. I asked her not the show me any gowns that were out of my price range. (I need to mention that I had been to this same bridal shop on many prior occasions for bridesmaid dresses for weddings that I had been in) The owner, Joyce, remembered me and commented that I was finally there for a wedding gown, instead of a bridesmaid's gown. So Joyce proceeded to bring out a number of gowns in the style I had requested. When I tried on "the one", I was afraid to ask how much. Joyce looks at the price tag and tells me, "for you $500.00". You know, I never did look at the price tag, I just knew God had given me favor that night. Janice and Patti were trying on different gowns, and they both tried on the same gown in two different color combinations! So we picked out my gown and theirs that night.

I remember lying in bed that night and thinking that all this couldn't be real. I just put down a $100.00 deposit on a wedding gown and was going to marry a man that I had only known for three months or so. The negative thoughts flooded my mind that Jim was going to change his mind, that someone was going to talk him out of it and that I was going to be the laughing stock of everyone's jokes. I prayed that God would help me fight those thoughts, and I soon felt peace in my heart.

In December, our church had a ladies' retreat at a retreat house set in the hills of Coventry, CT. The house was run by a Christian couple. Patti, myself and many of the women from our church attended the weekend retreat, as we had in the past years. We arrived Friday night and would stay until Sunday afternoon. It was always a wonderful time of fellowship for us women and a time to grow closer to the Lord. On Saturday morning we were enjoying the usual breakfast feast, and all the ladies were teasing me that this was my last retreat as a single woman. Out of the blue, our host Mike sits down next to me and says to me "Did your father ever tell you how beautiful you are?" I was like, "okay, who set him up to say this to me"? The ladies who knew me and knew my past history with my dad just looked as shocked as I was to hear him say that. I just simply said, "No" and continued to eat my breakfast. While we were cleaning up the breakfast dishes, Mike again comes up to me and says that he would like to talk to me. I can remember having this sinking feeling in the pit of my stomach that I was not going to like what this man was going to say to me.

So, Mike and I go into the sun room and sit down. Mike sat across from me and took my hands in his and looked me straight in the eyes and asked me again if my dad ever told me how beautiful I was. I just sat there with tears streaming down my face and asked him why he would ever think of asking me that question. Mike tells me that while we were eating breakfast, the Lord put on his heart that he needed to ask me that question. I sat there sobbing and began to tell him how it was just the opposite with my dad. Mike then asked me if Jim ever told me that I was beautiful, and I told him that Jim told me that all the time. Mike than asked me if I believed Jim when he said that to me. Again, still sobbing I said that I really didn't believe him, but I knew that Jim loved me and told me that out of his love for me. Mike then tells me that I was a beautiful woman whom God loves very much and that God wanted me to make peace with my dad before I married Jim. Suddenly the tears dried up and my guard went up and I asked Mike exactly what he felt God wanted me to do. Mike told me that the Lord showed him that my dad never told me that I was pretty and that my dad and I did not have a very good father/daughter relationship. I told Mike that I had been out on my own for nine years, and that I was over all that happened between my dad and me. Mike assured me that there was still a lot of hurt and bitterness in my heart towards my dad, and he told me that before I married Jim, I needed to ask my dad for forgiveness for holding bitterness and anger in my heart against him. Mathew 6:14-15 says "For if you forgive others, your Heavenly Father will forgive you. But if you do not forgive others of their sins, then your Father will not forgive your sins ". I just wanted to get up and run out of the room, because this guy was crazy! But, in my heart, I knew he was right and Mike and I prayed together that God would show me the right time and way to go and approach my dad about this. Needless to say, I had a very heavy heart after that.

Later that afternoon, I shared with the ladies all that Mike and I had talked about, and they all agreed that the Lord had definitely given Mike a word for me. Everyone gathered around me and laid their hands on me and prayed for the Lord to give me the strength and courage to do this to set myself free. See when you harbor unforgiveness and bitterness in your heart against anyone, it hurts you, not the person you are holding it against. I left the retreat knowing that I had less than four months to do this, and struggled within my heart, how I would ever be able to.

I came up with every excuse possible. I shared everything that Mike and I talked about with my mom, and she agreed that it was the right thing to do and she encouraged me to do it for myself. So one Sunday afternoon when I was visiting my parents, my dad was alone in the living room and I said down next to him and asked him if I could talk to him. My dad looked at me funny and said, "what do you want". I thought, "Here we go, he is already getting cocky with me and I didn't even say anything yet." So, I told my dad that I never felt that he loved me growing up, and that I wanted him to forgive me for holding anger and bitterness in my heart towards him because of that. My dad looked at me with a straight face and said, "You were a good girl, you didn't need love. You didn't give me any trouble like the other kids." I just sat there trying to absorb what he just said to me. I said, "Dad you're saying that I didn't need or deserve love because I was a good girl?" He sat straight up in his chair and looked at me and said harshly, "What do you want from me Mary Jane"?" I sat there choking back the tears that I just wanted him to forgive me for holding bitterness and anger in my heart against him, and he says "Okay". That was it, nothing else. I went back in the kitchen, still holding back the tears, and told my mother what happened. My mom told me that I did what God told me to do, and not to worry about anything else. I knew she was right, but I was still hurt and angry that I made myself venerable AGAIN with my dad.

Mike had asked me to call him when I finally did speak to my dad, so when I got home I called him. Thank God he was available because by this time I was sobbing and Mike told me that God would honor what I did. Mike told me that God would work on my dad's heart now, and that I had released all the years of bitterness and unforgiveness, and now satan had no stronghold on me in that area of my life. We prayed before we hung up, and Mike encouraged me to pray that the Lord would minister to my dad because hurting people, hurt people and my dad had his own issues that needed to be dealt with. I would love to say that I an overflowing sense of peace and joy immediately filled my heart, but it didn't. However, I loved the Lord with all my heart and I knew that He was pleased with me and I trusted the Lord to do the rest.

I want to mention what it means when I am saying that Mike received a word from the Lord. The Lord uses people to minister to each of us in this world. Many times the Lord will put a thought or an idea into someone's heart/mind, a thought that comes out of nowhere, but a thought that you just know is from God. When Mike told me God spoke to him and to ask me that question, the Lord knew that I would know that Mike would have never known to ask me that if He didn't give Mike those words. It is also referred to having a word of wisdom or knowledge.

I wish I could say that the following months were joyous, but they were everything but. My father made sure he told me that he just spent all his savings on my brother, Jimmy's wedding, and that he probably wouldn't even be able to give us a wedding present, let alone help us out with our wedding. My dad suggested that we postpone the wedding for a year or two so he could save money to help us. I told my dad that Jim and I each had money in our savings accounts, and that we would keep the wedding simple and within our budget. My dad was not happy with that at all. Not long after our engagement, I received a call one morning from the Psychiatric Ward at the local hospital that my dad had admitted himself for depression. I went to see him and he told me that he got extremely nervous about having to take care of my mother by himself. I knew in my heart right away, that the whole thing was his attempt to somehow get me to put off my wedding. A day or two later, I picked up my dad from the hospital and brought him home. I told him that I would try to help in any way that I could, but that he needed to hire more visiting nurses if he had to. I was so hurt and angry at him, that I just dropped him off without even going in to see my mom because I know she would have seen right through me and would know that my dad had again upset me.

Also, during that time my sister, Janice, was going through a difficult time in her marriage and had come to see one of the attorneys I worked for to possibly start divorce proceedings. (Fortunately, she and her husband worked things out before the wedding) The worst thing that happened, though, was that Patti's step-father died in January. He had been sick for some time, but died suddenly in his sleep one night. I had grown close to Patti's step-father over the years, he was like the father that I never had. He was very loving and generous to me. It was a very sad time for both Patti and me. My mom's health took another turn for the worse in March, and she ended up back in the hospital for some time.

At the time, our church was meeting in a school gym, and we used a local Christian church for all of our events such as weddings, showers, baptisms, etc. Well, as my luck would have it, in March (one month before our wedding) our Pastor and the Pastor of the church planned on getting married in had a falling out, and we would no longer be able to use their church facility for any of our events. Our invitations had already gone out and now we were in a predicament of having to find another church to get married in, as well as having to send out new invitations and directions. Thank God a couple in our church contacted Jim and I immediately and said that they were offering to pay for any printing and mailing costs that we would incur to send out new invitations and directions. Another couple suggested that we print up a letter stating the change of the church and the directions, and that is what we did. However, we first had to find another church. Patti had been going to a singles group at another Christian church in town and she called the Pastor of that church and he agreed to let us have our wedding there. The only problem was that that church had a very large staircase at the entrance, and my mom would not be able to get up the steps. All of our brothers and sisters at our church promised that they would provide a wheelchair for my mom and the guys would carry her in the wheelchair up the steps to get her there.

Talk about stress. At this point, I didn't even want a wedding, but Jim wouldn't have it any other way. I hated to have to tell my dad about it, because he would just say that he told me to wait, etc. My mom did her best to encourage me, and asked me to not let my dad get to me.

In late January, Jim took a job about 40 minutes out of Waterbury, and because of that bad weather, he started sleeping at my parents' house during the week. At this time, my parents had two empty bedrooms in their house. My dad charged Jim $25.00 a week to stay there, and after a few weeks, he started complaining that Jim used too much water taking showers and doing his laundry. (Mind you Jim took one shower a day and washed one load of clothes per week) We had been looking at apartment for us, and thank God one of our clients at the office had an apartment for rent that he recently remodeled, and Jim moved into the apartment in early March.

The weeks before the wedding were a blur. My sister, Phyllis, came home from Nebraska. Patti and the bridal party gave me a beautiful bridal shower. I had been packing my things and bringing them over to our apartment after work. It was an exciting time, yet it was emotionally drained for all the ups and downs that past months had been.

Well, it was finally the morning of April 21, 1990, our wedding day, and it was raining. I knew what that meant mom would not be able to come to the wedding. Because of her emphyzema and congestive heart failure, it was very difficult for my mom to breathe in rainy weather. My dad called me to let me know that mom wasn't going to be able to go to the church. I was very disappointed to say the least, but I knew that she couldn't and I asked to talk with her and I assured her that I understood and that I would come by the house right after the wedding so she could see me, Jim and the rest of the bridal party.

Our wedding was beautiful, the music was perfect and our Pastor gave an awesome message. After the ceremony, Jim and I and the entire wedding party stopped by to see my mom. She was shocked to see all of us. We all gathered around her bed and she said that she was so happy to see us and said to me that she was now at peace knowing that all her children were married and happy.

Our reception was awesome, I just wish I could remember everything. When you get married you are so busy greeting everyone and taking pictures, etc. that the day flies by. Thank God for our video and our pictures!! Anyway, it was a very happy day for Jim and me. We went back to our apartment and said our goodbyes to Patti. I knew Patti was happy for us, but it was also sad to know that she was going to be alone. We spent the night in a hotel next to the airport and left the following morning for our honeymoon cruise to Mexico.

We got back from our honeymoon on Friday, April 27th, the day before my birthday. It all still seemed so surreal. Our apartment was not far from the apartment that Patti and I shared before I got married. I would love to say the honeymoon continued for weeks and weeks on end, but sad to say the reality hit.

Monday morning came and Jim and I began getting ready for work. We were both working full time and had different routines in the morning. Jim had expectations for me as his wife that I was not ready to assume. Jim thought that I would get up, make him breakfast, make his lunch for work and send him off like a good wife should. I had my morning routine, which did not include any of those wifely duties. Needless to say, adjustments needed to be made. Jim had been living with his grandmother before we were married, and I guess she sometimes made him breakfast and put together a lunch for him. However, she was retired and had nothing else to do in the morning. Jim also expected a hot meal every night after work, which meant that I now had to plan meals for a week, something I definitely was not used to doing. I was good with a salad or a sandwich for supper, but that wasn't going to fly with Jim.

On top of the morning routines being somewhat a problem, I now inherited extra laundry that had to be done, grocery shopping to be planned and shopped for, etc. I guess we never really discussed all these household chores. I assumed that everything would be shared like it was when Patti and I were roommates. Jim had the assumption that I was automatically going to become the Psalms 31 wife, who was completely submissive and devoted to her husband. Hello? Let the fights begin.

It took some time before Jim and I reached a happy medium. I still felt that I was doing way more than my share. The church we were attending at the time was full of dominating males and submissive females, so I didn't get much help there. Patti's only comment was, "Well I'm glad you prayed harder than me for a husband". Thanks Patti. Thank God I had my sister, Janice, to bounce things off of. Janice had already been married for a few years and had two children by this time, so she always knew how I felt. Janice always seemed to know just what to say when I started complaining about all that "I" was expected to do. She was more like a mother to me back then in a weird sort of way.

In August of 1990, my mother's health took a turn for the worse. It was getting too hard for her to breathe on her own and the doctor decided that she should hospitalized and hooked up to a ventilator. Mom hated being hooked up to the ventilator and her hands had to be tied to the side rails so she would not pull it out. I was working full time at the law firm at the time, and I would do all my work and then leave for the day to spend time with my mom. The doctors kept telling us that she was probably not going to survive without being on a respirator. We all knew that that that was not the kind of life our mother would want to live. My attorney had drawn up living wills for my parents when he did their Wills and he told me that I had better get my mother's living will out and give it to the hospital. As luck would have it, I was designated to be the one to make the decision to "pull the plug" if the doctors deemed her to be terminal. One afternoon my sister Janice and I were visiting her and mom got into a couching fit and somehow coughed out the ventilator tube. The doctors and nurses were shocked because they had never seen a patient do that. Thus came the moment of truth, do we tell the doctors to put the tube back in or leave it out and see if mom could breathe on her own. All of us got together at the hospital that evening and decided that we would leave it in God's hands. We knew that mom would never want to live here life intubated, but we were told that it was very unlikely that mom could last very long breathing on her own. We decided that we would not intubate her and see what happens. My father trusted our decision. The next day I visited mom and she was very weak. She told me that she prayed that she would go home to be with the Lord and asked me why He wasn't taking her. I told her that He will in His time. As much as I hated to see my mother suffering, I still was believing for a miracle. Two days later, on August 22, 1990, we received a call in the middle of the night that mommy had died. It was the saddest day of my life and all our lives. Mom was the rock in the family, she was the glue that held us together. We all went over to her house every Sunday and had pizza with her and dad. Sundays would never be the same, and they never were.

CHAPTER 6

By December of 1990, I found out that I was pregnant with our first child. This is when the trials really came. Within the first few weeks of my pregnancy, I began having severe morning sickness, which lasted throughout the day. It was so awful that I couldn't get ready for work without vomiting a couple of times. When I got home from work the last thing I wanted to do was make dinner. All the different smells would make me vomit. By the second month of my pregnancy, I couldn't even keep water down and I eventually got severely dehydrated and had to be hospitalized for a week or so.

At the same time, my good friend from church, Judy, was pregnant with her third child and was experiencing the same severe morning sickness as I was. We tried everything to try to keep from vomiting. Thank God we had each other at the time because it was so difficult to go through, so physically draining and emotionally challenging, that I know I would have never have had the strength to go through that time without her prayers and the prayers of others. By the fourth month of my pregnancy, in April of 1991, the morning sickness finally started to subside and I began to finally gain weight. I continued working full time in the law firm right up to a couple of weeks before I was due. Jim and I had decided that I would be a stay home mom and raise our child. A month before my due date, Jim got laid off from his job. My boss was excited because he thought that meant that I would have my baby and come back to work. I remember having the conversation with my boss that God would provide for us, and that we have made our decision and we were not changing our minds. Thank God that Jim's insurance was going to stay in effect for a couple of months, so we didn't have that worry.

On Labor Day evening I began having contractions in the middle of the night. I remember laying on the couch watching the Jerry Lewis Telethon and trying to keep track of how long the contractions were lasting. By morning, we contacted the doctor and we were told to head to the hospital as soon as the contractions got five minutes apart. By evening that day, Jim brought me to the hospital. Once I was examined, it was learned that I was only 1 centimeter, but they felt it best to admit me, as things could change at any moment. Jim and my sister, Janice, said their goodbyes for the night and told me to call if anything changed.

It was about 3:00 a.m. and all of the sudden I felt excrutiating cramps and pain like I had never felt before. I buzzed the nurse and she informed me that I was now in labor and that I was going to be moved to the delivery room. I remember thinking that if this was the beginning of labor, what was I in for? I called Jim and Janice and they came as quickly as they could.

I was in labor for about eight hours, when they finally gave me an epidural. As soon as I got the epidural, I fell asleep. The next thing I knew my doctor was waking me up to tell me that my baby was in fetal distress and that he had to perform an emergency C-section. The nurses wheeled me out of the room and into the operating room. I was crying and asking for Jim, but there was no time to talk. As soon as I was wheeled into the operating room, the doctor cut me open and delivered my baby in four minutes! The nurses told me that the baby had been forced into the canal, but I was not dilating, so she was losing oxygen and had to be delivered immediately to avoid any brain damage. Thank God, Christina Amelia Robinson, was born healthy and strong with no medical problems.

By the time Jim was able to change into scrubs and join me in the operating room, the nurses were cleaning Christina and wrapping her up in her little cocoon. The nurse handed Christina to Jim and he brought her over to me so I could see her. It truly was a miracle in every sense of the word.

I had already decided before Christina was born that I was going to breastfeed her. The nurse came into my room a couple of hours later, and began to show me how to breastfeed. I was so engourged at the time I thought my poor baby was going to suffocate while trying to nurse. After a few days, we both got the hang of it and I was already beginning to feel like a pro. Wow, motherhood had now begun. Scary and exciting at the same time.

When Jim and I first found out that I was pregnant, we discussed what we were going to do about my job. Both Jim and I did not want to put our infant into a day care facility. I wasn't earning very much at the time and we decided that it would be almost a wash for me to continue working and paying daycare. As my pregnancy neared the final months, I broke the news to my boss that I was going to quit working after I had my baby and be a stay home mom. My boss made the comment, "Jim must make a lot of money for you to do that". I assured him that we would be making a sacrifice, but day care was out of the question. About a month before my due date, Jim got laid off from his job. My boss was certain that I was going to change my mind and continue to work, but I told him that I was still going to quit once the baby was born. Jim and I had faith that God would provide for us no matter what. My boss was completely at a loss for words, but in my heart I knew we could do this.

Needless to say, Jim found another job about a week before Christina was born. Jim was able to cobra his medical insurance from his prior job, so we had complete insurance coverage for my delivery and for the baby.

Once we got into a daily routine with Christina, we got more and more comfortable with parenthood. I think the hardest part was making the adjustment of going from working a full time job for over 10 years to staying home every day. When you become a mom, at least for me, you begin to lose your identity. The days all seemed to be the same. I stopped putting my contacts in, I wore the same clothes, kept my hair tied up, etc. My appearance was not important like it was when I was working in the office. I nursed Christina for a full year, without any supplements. My breast milk was so rich, that she was nice and chunky and my pediatrician didn't want me to introduce anything else but water to her diet. I was doing my best to be a good "Christian" mother and wife. It was the hardest job I ever had.

Money was tight during that time and I went back to work at the law firm at night. My boss gave me keys to the building and the elevator, and I would work from 7:30 to 11:30, two or three nights a week. It was nice to have some spending money in my pocket, and it was good to get out of the house and keep up my skills at the office. It worked out good for the law firm as well, because I would be able to put out a lot of work in those few hours, without any interruptions. (other than calls from my husband freaking out cause the baby wouldn't stop crying for some reason or another) I knew my job well enough that I could do most of the work without any supervision or direction.

Most of my friends who had children put their children into day care, and resumed their jobs a few months after their babies were born. Luckily, my sister, Janice, was also a stay home mom and we used to talk for hours on the phone. She had two older children and a young son. There was one friend, Judy, from church who was a stay home mom like me, and we would spend many hours during the week praying for each other. We both had very demanding children and husbands. Jim thought he "worked all day", so he didn't really want to have to "babysit" the baby when I went to work. I know those reading this can already see what most of our arguments were about!

Well a couple of years went by and we decided to try for a second child. Within a few months, I was pregnant with our second child in June of 1993. My morning sickness wasn't as bad as it was with Christina, but I still had it for the first four months. Christina was a very strong willed child, and it was very difficult trying to keep up with her while feeling sick to my stomach.

We were still living in our apartment when I got pregnant with our second child, and we knew that we would have to start looking for a house. In November 1993, we moved into our first home in a nice section in Waterbury. It was an older home that was built in the late 1950s, with oak floors throughout, a fireplace and a very private back yard. However, the house was still in the 1950's on the inside and needed to be remodeled. Jim decided that he would do all of the remodeling himself, room by room. He tore up all the wall to wall carpet and the oak underneath was like brand new. Everything in the house was dark brown and gold, but there was much potential, we knew we could make it "our" home. Since money was tight, the remodeling took many years to complete.

On February 11, 1994, in the middle of a huge snow storm, I went into labor with our second child. Everyone was sure that we were having a boy, but we had another girl, Alaina Chrysoula Robinson. I could not deliver Alaina naturally, and needed to have another C-section. Jim's grandmother came down to take care of Christina (and Jim) while I was in the hospital, and left when I got back home. I nursed Alaina, took care of a very demanding two year old, kept up all the household chores, put dinner on the table every night and went back to working in the office at night. The days were very full, I was averaging 4 hours of sleep at night and my patience was wearing thin. Jim couldn't seem to understand why I wasn't all "fixed" up when he got home from work. These years really tested our commitment to each other, believe me. Also, during the years when our children were young, my husband changed jobs or got laid off numerous times, which left us with lapse of money and medical insurance. I hated not having stability in our home and I was angry at my husband because of his job situations. There were many nights that I would be so sick and tired of "giving" and "doing" for everyone else, that I would type my own divorce complaint and leave it on the kitchen table for Jim to sign in the morning. Needless to say that God convicted me of this, and I knew I had to start really praying for myself, my children and my marriage. My friend, Judy, was going through the same exact circumstances, and we were strong for each other. When I was weak in my faith and frustrated with life, Judy would be strong and convince me that I couldn't let the devil tear apart my marriage and my family. When Judy was having a hard time, I would encourage her the same way.

Any wives and mothers reading this and who are struggling with demands of motherhood, working or whatever, you need a good friend that you can vent with, who can encourage you and who can keep you on track. Judy is still my very close friend, now we just share our teenage woes with each other. We used to say we couldn't wait for our kids to grow up, but the problems just got bigger as they got older.

In November 2004 when Alaina was nine months old, I found out that I was pregnant again. I remember the day like it was yesterday. I took a home pregnancy test and it showed positive for pregnancy. I started crying and shaking the test and Christina came into the bathroom to see what was wrong. She saw me crying and shaking test and she says, "Don't worry mommy, daddy can fix it." I looked up at her and told her "Daddy cannot fix this". I knew she had no idea what was going on, but she was so cute I just had to hug her and tell her that everything was all right. I was so at my wits end with the girls and life in general, that I wouldn't tell anyone that I was pregnant except for my sister, Janice, Judy and Patti. I was so upset that I was pregnant again that I prayed to God that I would have a miscarriage. Abortion was never an option, but I was struggling with the thought of another child at home.

It just so happened that Alaina was due for her nine month checkup that afternoon. My pediatrician was a Christian and I considered her more like a friend because she would always take the time to give me a "mommy checkup" when I would bring my children to her office. Dr. Mahooti was a very godly woman and she had a lot of wisdom, and she would encourage me whenever I saw her. That day as she was checking Alaina, she told me that I was getting too skinny and needed to eat more. I said to her "Well I won't be skinny for long because I'm pregnant." Before I could finish my sentence I began to cry, and told her that I didn't want any more children because I couldn't handle the two I already had. She hugged me and told me that she knew exactly how I felt because when she thought she was done having children, and then found out she was pregnant with her fifth child. She got teary eyed and confessed that being a doctor herself that she could have terminated the baby without anyone ever knowing, but she knew that God would know, so she couldn't. I told her that I was going to pray that I would just have a miscarriage, and that way it would have been God's will. Dr. Mahooti told me that her fifth child was a boy, and that God was giving me a son. She left the room and came back with a copy of a letter that her son, who was now in college, wrote to her a year ago. She told me to read it when I had a chance and hugged me and told me that God would work everything out for His good.

When Jim got home from work that evening, I broke the news to him. He was actually happy because he wanted more children. When I had Alaina, I wanted to have my tubes tied while the doctor still had me open, but Jim would not agree. Jim saw how upset I was and kept saying it was all his fault, but we both knew that was not true. I told Jim that I didn't want our families to know until I could talk about it without crying!!! That night, I had a chance to read the letter that Dr. Mahooti gave me. It was a letter that her son wrote to her thanking her for bringing him into this world and raising him to love God because he wanted to work in the mission field and help others like his mother. It was so touching and I tried so hard to be happy about being pregnant, but all I could do was think about how I was going to do it. In my mind, the easy way out would be that I would have a miscarriage and then get my tubes tied and then no more worries!

We spent Christmas day home that year because I wasn't feeling great. Morning sickness had begun and I was literally too sick and tired. That evening as I was sleeping in bed I started having what I thought were labor pains. I woke Jim and told him that something was wrong. I could hardly get up and walk, but I knew I needed to go to the Emergency Room as quickly as possible. We called Patti and she came right over to watch the girls. I thought for sure that I was having a miscarriage, and then this awful sadness came over me because I remembered that a miscarriage was what I had asked God for. I didn't mention any of this to Patti or Jim. When we arrived at the hospital, we told them that I was pregnant and having severe pain and they took me right in. After some tests, it was revealed that I had a kidney stone, and I would need to stay the night. The doctor told me that I was also very dehydrated, and he was concerned that there may not be enough fluid in my placenta and he wanted to do an ultrasound in the morning to make sure the baby was all right.

I couldn't sleep all night between the physical pain and the pain in my heart that my unborn child's life may be in danger. I kept thinking about all the messages that I had heard about making sure what you ask God for, because it may not always be His best. So, I laid there asking God to forgive me and to let my child be okay. In the morning, I was told that I would have to pass the stone on my own because I was pregnant. Then came time for the ultrasound. My heart was pounding because I knew if my baby was in danger, it was my fault. The nurse put the ultrasound on my stomach and asked me the sex of my children at home. I told her that I had two girls ages 3 and nine months. She looked at the doctor and then back at me and said, "Well you finally got your little boy." I was afraid to ask if he was okay, and before I could, the doctor told me that everything was fine and he was doing great. I laid there and sobbed and everyone thought they were tears of joy, but really I was crying from the thought that I had prayed for my little boy's life to end.

My pregnancy went well after that, however, I was told that I could not nurse Alaina anymore because of my morning sickness. The nursing and vomiting were what caused me to get dehydrated and thus get a kidney stone. It was very difficult to just stop nursing Alaina. When I nursed my children, my breast milk was so rich, that I did not need to supplement their diet for the first year of their life. I was sad that I had to give Alaina formula and she was not happy to have it, but she was actually ready for baby food, so it helped with the transition.

I had to switch gynocologists because of insurance reasons, and my new doctor told me that he was going to schedule a C-section. My section was scheduled for June 27, 2005, however, Zachary James Robinson, decided he wanted to arrive early, so on June 22, 2005, Zachary was born. When my girls were born, I was not able to hold them after they were delivered. Christina was taken immediately for tests, and I had to go under anesthesia with Alaina because my epidural wore off. So I wanted to be awake and be able to hold my child, because I was having my tubes tied right that same day and it was my last chance to hold my newborn baby. Well as my luck would have it, the epidural would not take and I was given two options, go under anesthesia or have a spinal tap. I chose the spinal tap, which left me unable to move any part of my body, except my head. Therefore, I wasn't able to hold Zachary for many hours after he was delivered.

We brought Zachary home, and the girls were all excited to see their baby brother. The first night home I was sleeping in bed and I had the most unbelievable pain in my stomach. I woke Jim and we called the doctor and were told to go to his office first thing in the morning for a checkup. When the doctor saw me and started to examine my incision, and the area where I was having pain, and he decided that I may have some kind of infection and I would need to go back in the hospital for a couple of days so that he could keep an eye on me. By the time I arrived at the hospital, I had a fever of 105, and I was shivering uncontrollably. I was wheeled right in and blood tests were started. I was given medication for the pain and for the fever and Jim was told that he better go get some formula because I would not be able to nurse Zachary while I was on medication. Zachary was not even a week old and Jim had to call his sister to bring his grandmother down to watch the girls so he could go to work. My sister, Janice, watched Zachary during the day. After a couple of days in the hospital, I began to get worse. My fever would not go down, I couldn't keep anything down and the pain was getting worse. I was worried my breast milk would dry up, so the nurses would pump my breasts throughout the day. I was a mess and no one had any answers as to why.

On the fourth day at the hospital, a women comes to see me and introduces herself as the head of the Infectious Disease Control Department and told me that I had e-coli in my blood, and the doctors were doing their best to kill the bacteria. I freaked out and asked her how this could happen to me, as I was healthy when I delivered Zachary. She tried to calm me down and stated that e-coli lives in our intestines and that maybe the doctor nicked my intestines when he made the incision. I called Janice and Jim and told them the news. I forgot to mention that my dad would come to visit me almost daily and would sit in my room and complain to me how no one comes to visit him or calls to check on him. It got to the point that I had the nurse put a NO VISITORS sign on my door. I felt so lousy and was depressed enough without having to hear my Dad complain about stupid stuff to me.

After a week of multiple antibiotics being pumped into me to no avail, a doctor came in to visit me and told me that they could not find when the bacteria was festering, and that they decided that they were going to give me a hysterectomy! I totally freaked out and started screaming and crying and told him that he was absolutely not giving me a hysterectomy, that I came into the hospital healthy and that someone or something was dirty and now I was infected with e-coli. I called Jim to get to the hospital as quick as he could. I threw the doctor out of my room and demanded that someone figure out how to make me better. Suddenly a woman comes in and introduces herself as the hospital counselor and asked me if I wanted to talk to her. Was she kidding?? Talk to her, I wanted to kill her and everyone else!

The whole time I had been in the hospital my church was praying for me and my pastor visited me, but my faith was very weak. I could not imagine why God was not healing me. Jim was a wreck trying to work, drop Zak off every morning, come to see me, take care of the girls, etc. Jim asked the pastor to call the church to pray that whatever was causing the e-coli to fester, that the doctors would find it and take care of the problem. The very next day, my incision brew up like a big red orange and the doctor came in and told me that he would have to reopen my incision to take out the abscess. The doctor said he would reopen my incision right there in my bed, while I was awake. The nurse gave me a couple of needles in the area around my incision to numb it, and the doctor removed the abscess. The area where the e-coli was growing was finally found and taken care of, thank God. Within a few days, I felt well enough to go home, and Jim needed to be taught how to clean and care for my incision. I finally was released from the hospital on July 8, 2005, which was my mother's birthday. I knew God had heard the prayers of my brothers and sisters at church, and I was happy be able to see my children.

Once I was home and feeling better and returned to work, the big question came "Well are you going to sue the hospital for this?" I received this question from family members, friends and from the attorney that I worked for. It was a clear cut and dry lawsuit against the hospital, nurses and the doctor who delivered Zachary, however, as a Christian, I wasn't exactly clear as to what God wanted me to do. I did spend three weeks of hell in the hospital, my husband missed many days of work and we had three children that we needed to find care for, but I prayed and asked God to heal me and he did. The deciding factor came from my very Godly pediatrician. Dr. Mahooti was the pediatrician for all three of my children. She was more than a doctor to me, she was a very dear and trusted friend. I brought Zachary for one of his appointments and Dr. Mahooti came right out and asked me if I was considering a lawsuit against the my doctor and the hospital. I told her that I had been asked that question from everyone and I just wasn't exactly sure what I should do. Dr. Mahooti proceeded to tell me that my gynecologist was a very good man and that she knew for a fact that he was at the hospital every day checking on me. She also told me that a malpractice suit against him would be devastating to him and his practice. Dr. Mahooti explained what I knew already that I would have to bring the lawsuit against him and the hospital. Because I trusted Dr. Mahooti so much and I knew she was right and I decided right then and there that I was not going to start any lawsuit for damages (even though I knew it could have been an easy six figure win). I knew that Dr. Mahooti was speaking God's word to me to forgive and forget. I was completed recovered, my baby was doing fine and my family life was back in order.

This can also be a word to anyone reading this book, if you have been through a similar situation when you have been injured or became ill from no fault of your own, please think twice before you run and seek legal advice. Our society is so quick to sue each other, which results in insurance rates sky rocketing. Can we all try to live honestly and if we are injured or made ill, yet we fully recover, let us not be quick to sue for damages. The only real winners in all these lawsuits are the attorneys who take the cases.

CHAPTER 7

FOR THE NEXT FIVE YEARS I continued as a stay home mom with our three children. It was in those five years that my faith as put to the ultimate test. I had three children in five years. I used to kid and say that I worked at a day-care all day and no one ever came to pick up their child. I continued to work part time at the law firm in the evenings. I put dinner on the table every night, cleaned, shopped, went to doctor visits, had play dates at the park at least once a week and tried to be the best Christian mother I could be. My children and my husband were all very demanding of my time and I was losing my identity. During these years, our marriage was tried and tested. In those years, we only had a landline phone and when I needed to talk to an adult, I would either call one of my sisters or my friend, Judy. If it were not for those conversations, I honestly think I would have given up on my marriage. Jim expected dinner on the table every night and wanted the kids to stay quiet while he took his nap before dinner. Try keeping three small children quiet, while you try to cook dinner. You guessed it, many arguments over this. One the nights that I had to work, I needed to have them bathed and ready for bed before I went to work. You guessed it, many arguments over this. When I was at work, I would get at least one or two calls from my husband about who was crying, who would not go to sleep or who wanted something to eat. I would tell him that I could not call him during the day to complain about the children's behavior and he couldn't call me at night while I worked. The arguments got more and more frequent and more and more ugly. Many nights I would type a Divorce Complaint and leave it on the kitchen table for him to see in the morning.

I had the perfect marriage, home and children on the outside, but on the inside, we had our problems. I knew we were not alone in our problems, but that didn't help how I was feeling.

During this time our pastor's wife gave me a cassette (yes that long ago) of a Christian preacher, Joyce Meyer. She suggested that I listen to her because she really had an anointed ministry. I listened to the tape over and over again. Joyce Meyer was such an encouragement to me. Shortly after, I learned that she had televised programs on TV and I was able to watch her now and then. I can honestly say that Joyce's ministry had a huge impact on my life. Her teaching was so basic and timely for me that I found that my faith was strengthened by her teachings. One day Joyce shared how difficult her marriage was in the beginning. Joyce shared that she had a lot of hurt and bitterness in her heart from years of sexual abuse by her father and a lot of her hurt and bitterness flowed into her marriage. Joyce shared that her husband, Dave, wanted to divorce her many times because she was so difficult to live with. Joyce shared that Dave went for counselling was told that he needed to stick it out with her because Joyce was going to become an international preacher and she could not become all that God wanted her to be without his help. That word stuck with me and convicted me. I felt the Lord speaking to my heart that I couldn't divorce Jim because whatever God's plan for our lives was, that it would not come into fruition if we didn't stay together. From that day on, I promised the Lord that I would not type another divorce complaint and no entertain that option.

Around this time, a group of stay home moms started to exercise a couple of times a week at our church. We had a TaeBo video and we would bring our children and let them play in the nursery while we exercised. It was a double blessing. We had fellowship and prayer time and we got in shape. We continued this for a few years. Fellowship with good friends and exercise are the best things anyone could do to keep mentally and physically fit. However, even with all that, I found myself struggling each day to get up and push myself to take care of my children, my home and my husband. Nothing in my life was ever easy. I was very sleep deprived, as there on always at least one child up a couple of time in the night and since my husband had to get up for work, I was always the one to tend to the child that was up crying and fussing. My children were all very strong willed, and even the simplest things were a battle. I felt that I was fighting to keep control of the children, fighting to not give in to their demands and fighting not to want to just leave and let someone else deal with them.

I spoke to my pediatrician at one of my children's appointments, and I asked her if she could prescribe something for my children so they would sleep through the night and be less demanding during the day. She laughed and told me that I was the one who needed medication. She gave me the analogy of a broken leg needing a cast and my mind being broken and needing medication. I thought she was out of HER mind. I'm fine---it's THEM!!!!! She asked me to promise her that I would go to see my primary care physician and let him decide. I agreed that I would do that, but I honestly had no intention of actually calling him. I was thinking, she must be CRAZY, I just need the children to be less strong willed and to sleep through the night so I could get my rest. I talked to Jim about what my pediatrician had said, and he said that that was a very stupid idea. I spoke to some of my other Christian stay home moms and was told that I just needed to pray and ask God to give me the strength to get through the day. Now on top of everything else, I'm feeling like a failure because I wasn't trusting God enough and not turning over call my cares to Him.

Taking antidepressants was not very popular back in the 90s. Even my best friend, Judy, didn't think that taking medication was the answer. However, the overwhelming feelings of frustration, exhaustion and the loss of appetite was evident. I honestly did not feel that I needed anything, I thought that if the pediatrician could just give my three children something to "calm them down" that everything would be all right.

After much thought, prayer and discussion, I finally made an appointment with my primary physician for a checkup. I told him everything that had been going on and how I was feeling. My doctor listened intently as I poured my heart out to him. When I was done he looked at me and told me that I needed antidepressants. I asked him how he knew that. He told me that normally he would do a test to check my serotonin levels, but after listening to me, he knew that I was suffering from depression. I insisted that I was not depressed, I was frustrated, angry, tired and disgusted with everything and everyone, but I WAS NOT DEPRESSED!! He told me that all those feelings are signs and symptoms of depression and he was sure that I needed to be put on an antidepressant. He prescribed one for me and told me that I should start feeling better within two weeks.

For some reason, I was embarrassed that I was put on an antidepressant. In my mind, when someone is depressed they lay in bed all day, don't participate in normal daily events and shut themselves out from everyone. I wasn't depressed, I got up every day, took care of three children, did laundry, cooked meals, etc. I never stopped. However, I trusted my doctor and decided to give it a chance because I wanted to feel better about being a mother and a wife. To be perfectly honest, being a stay home mom is and was the hardest job that I have ever had. It is very mentally and physically draining and one of the most unthankful jobs one could ever have. I never regretted my decision and I loved my children, but it was very difficult at times. Many of my friends who decided to go back to work full time and put their children day care, would tell me how "lucky" I was to be a stay home mom. There was and is no luck involved. It is a sacrifice and a decision that we made as a couple, and we made the conscious decision to do so. Many times when the children were small, my husband was either laid off or switched jobs, and our income was down and we had no medical insurance for periods of time. Thank God that He kept me, my husband and our children healthy during those times. When the children did need to see the pediatrician, she would just charge me the normal co-pay for the visit. Dr. Mahooti was a beautiful Christian woman who loved her job and others. She taught me a lot in the years that I spent taking my children to her. She was truly a God send. I looked to her as a sort of mother and took her advice and trusted her judgment.

Two weeks went by and all that I noticed that was different was that I was gaining weight, and that was not something I wanted to do. I called my doctor and told him that I didn't want to continue taking the antidepressant. My doctor told me that I was going to get more depressed, and I told him that if I continue taking the antidepressant and gaining weight I'm going to get even more depressed. My doctor told me that there are many different antidepressants that he could prescribe, and he said he would put me on a different one that did not have weight gain as a side effect. Well, besides feeling nauseous for the first two weeks on the new antidepressant, I actually began to feels less frustrated, less agitated and calmer. My husband, friends and family still continued to tell me that they thought that I could have accomplished the same with God's help on my own. I finally got peace that I had tried my best to get through my days with prayer and trust in God, and that I was not a failure, I actually needed the medication, which soon was called "my happy pill". Sometimes, you just have to trust your doctor and your own heart in making some decisions. I wanted to be superwoman and supermom, but I forgot to take care of me. As in everything in life, there has to be balance in everything and we can't expect to run on empty and not have any problems.

As I mentioned before, me and a few the women from our church and some of our friends did Taebo a couple of times a week. One of the women who went was a pastor's wife from another church, who suggested that I go talk to someone to help me sort out my issues. Money was very tight back then, and I didn't want to incur any additional bills, so I wasn't sure how I was going to be able to get free counselling. At that time I had a friend, Mary Ann, who was going to the local women's shelter for counselling. She suggested that I could get free counseling at the women's shelter because the shelter was for all women who needed help. Well, I hesitated to call, but when I finally did, I was paired up with a counselor named Diane, who was a true God send to me. She got me to realize that I was being too hard on myself and also still suffering from the verbal abuse from my father. I was able to get past the hurt and pain still in my heart from my dad, and to begin to see myself as God sees me. I don't know how many months that I went to talk to Diane, but she helped build up my self-esteem, helped me to realize that I don't have to compare myself to anyone and that I should never let anyone tear me down.

Only a very few of my closest friends knew that I was counseling with Diane. I never told Jim because he never would agree to go counseling with me and he thought that if I was going to talk to anyone, I was probably complaining about him. I want to encourage any woman, wife or mother to find someone that you can trust to talk to. It doesn't mean that you are a failure if you need counseling or mental help, it just means that you have too much on your plate and you need some professional help to help you get your priorities in order and to get boundaries set in your life. I want to explain that I didn't tell Jim that I was going to Diane because he would automatically assume that I was going to her to talk about him and "blame" him for my problems. Jim has his own self esteem issues and he really needed to talk to someone about things that went on in his life, but he was totally against counseling and wouldn't even consider it. One thing that I have learned over the years is that we are only responsible for our own lives before God, and that we can't change anyone unless they want to change. Sometimes when we make changes in our lives and focus on that, the problems that we see in others don't seem that big after all. Let me encourage anyone reading this book that is struggling with personal issues to seek professional help and don't feel like a failure. If we don't love ourselves, then we cannot truly love others.

CHAPTER 8

In December of 1999, our oldest brother got divorced and moved in with dad in the family home. Dad had been asking one of us to build an in-law apartment for him to live in. He would sell his home and give the money to whoever would agree to build the apartment for him. Sadly, none of us took him up on the offer because none of us wanted to be told how to live our lives. Anyway, my brother decided to move in with dad and dad was happy not to be alone. Dad had a female companion at the time, but she was not the home body type. He took her out to eat all the time because she didn't cook and couldn't even make a pot of coffee. But, that was his business.

By January of 2000, Carl had convinced our dad to deed the family home over to him, so in the event dad had to be confined to a convalescent home, the State would not be able to take the home to pay for his stay. My dad had attempted to get the property out of his name years before, but my boss would not have the deed typed because my dad had stated that the reason for the transfer was mainly to hide the equity in the home from the State. So now Carl had an attorney who would do the deed for dad, and dad is asking me the ins and outs of such transfer. I told dad he needed to retain a "life use" in his house, so he can remain there and still retain title to the house. Dad stated that he wanted a clause put on the deed that if and when he dies, the property would be sold and divided amongst his then living children. I indicated to dad that the attorney will put any clause he asked for on the deed. A few weeks later, dad came to my house with a copy of the deed. Dad stated that my brother was insulted about the clause he wanted on the deed because it made him feel like dad didn't trust him, so the clause was left off. However, dad did have a clause added to the deed which stated that if my brother was to cohabit with a female in the family residence the deed would become "null and void". I asked my dad why he would put such a strange clause on the deed and he told me that he knows that my brother, a deacon in the Catholic Church, was secretly allowing his girlfriend spend the night at the house and he was totally against sex outside of marriage. I guess my dad would go to bed early when my brother and his girlfriend were still up and then when he would get up in the middle of the night, he would see her car still parked in front of the house. I told my dad that if he was sure that she was sleeping there, and he needs to speak to my brother, not to me.

In late February 2000, I received a call from my brother stating that dad was complaining of chest pains that morning before he left for work, and suggested that I check in on him. I tried calling dad's house, got his answering machine and I assumed he must have went to work. (We did not have cell phones at this time) A few hours later, my sister Janice called me to say that she received a call from the hospital and dad was brought in by ambulance earlier that day for a possible heart attack. Wow, my brother calls me to check on dad when he lives with him and knew how severe his chest pains must have been and decided to go to work anyway?? Surprising, but typical for my brother. By dinner time, we were all waiting to hear the results of the tests on dad, and I received a call from my brother. He said that he was going through dad's things and started listing one by one what each of us owed dad. I was floored! Especially, when he said I owed dad over $1,000 for my wedding, when dad did not pay one cent for my wedding and told me he didn't have anything to give for a gift!! Right then and there I knew my brother was up to something and I called my sister to tell her about the conversation, and she stated that my brother had already called her with the same accusations.

My sister and I went to see dad at the hospital and we learned that he had four blockages in his heart and would need a quadruple bypass operation in New Haven, CT as soon as possible. Since I had Power of Attorney in place for my dad, he asked me to get his check book and bills from the house and make sure his February bills got paid on time. My sister and I told dad about the calls we received from our brother, and dad stated that he was not surprised. I told dad that I didn't trust him, and dad asked me to go to his house and get all his banking information out of his desk and bring it to my house. I told him that I would. I told dad that our brother couldn't wait for him to die so he could get the house for himself. Dad shook his head and agreed.

Dad's quadruple by-pass operation was scheduled for Friday, February 25, 2000 at St. Raphael's Hospital in New Haven, CT. My three children were little at the time, so it was very difficult for me to go to the hospital without them, and they were too young for visitation. My sister and my brothers, Dan and Mike, went up to see dad the night after surgery. Dad was in ICU and very groggy. My sister said that our eldest brother went to see dad before them and when they went in the room after him, dad was sitting up in his bed with a shocked look on his face. They called for the nurse and the nurse told them that everyone had to leave because dad was very anxious and upset and they wanted him to rest. My sister told me that she never saw a look on dad the way he looked when they came into the room.

By Sunday, I was able to visit dad with my sister. He was very concerned that certain items in his home be taken out for safe keeping. He knew that he had to go to a rehabilitation facility for a while and wanted his valuables out of the house. We told him we would take them, but we never did because we thought he was just under the influence of the pain meds he was taking.

Dad became very depressed after his surgery, and the hospital staff kept asking us to try to talk to him, to cheer him up because he had made it through the most difficult part. We all tried different ways to try to get dad to talk and let us know why he was so depressed, but we just figured it was just the result of such a huge surgical procedure, and having to be confined to a hospital and a convalescent home for a undetermined amount of time. Dad was still working 40 plus hours with the Visiting Nurses Association and now he was not able to care for himself. We assumed that was why he was so depressed. When we couldn't visit, my sister, Janice, and I would talk to dad over the phone. Janice had a service on her phone that allowed three way calling. We would talk to dad and try our best to encourage him. I remember when we would say good bye my sister would say, "Bye dad. I love you" and he would say "Love you too". When I would say "Bye dad. I love you" I would just get a "Bye". I would be so sad that he could not tell me that he loved me and I had to fight back the old hurt that would try to come back. Bottom line was we just wanted dad to get better and come home, and that's all that mattered.

Sad to say that a few weeks after dad's surgery, his heart stopped and he passed away in the early morning hours of March 11, 2000. I can remember that day like it was yesterday. We all went to the convalescent home to say our good byes. Later that afternoon we all met at the family home to discuss when we would have the wake and funeral. Our sister, Phyllis, was living in Nebraska with her husband and two sons at the time, and we needed to give her time to fly home. We were discussing when she and her family would stay, and we all assumed that she would stay at dad's house, since there were two empty bedrooms. Immediately my oldest brother began making excuses why they could not stay there. He needed his privacy, he was too busy to help them out, and other lame excuses that none of us were buying. We all had our own families, and we had no room to put up four extra people. Dad's house was the most logical place for our sister and her family to stay, and finally, after much discussion, our eldest brother agreed she could stay at "his house". When we all heard him call the family home "his house", we all knew that something was very wrong. Then came the discussion of when to have the wake and funeral. Immediately our eldest brother said that he had a very important meeting on Friday, the day we all agreed would be the best day to have the funeral, and he could not cancel it. We all were working full time jobs at the time and we all had to request bereavement time off for the wake and funeral. He was adamant that his meeting could not be cancelled, and then our sister called and stated that she would be home Wednesday evening and would have to fly back on Saturday. Now it was definite that we had to wake dad that Thursday, and funeral on Friday. Our brother was beside himself that he would have to cancel this important meeting, but refused to discuss what the meeting was about that was so important. He was a Chaplin in the prison system and a deacon in a church, what could possibly be more important than your father's wake and funeral?? So after much discussion, it was settled that Phyllis and her family would stay at the family home and the wake and funeral would be Thursday and Friday of that week.

Being a deacon, our eldest brother said the mass at dad's funeral. Our youngest brother, Jimmy, had prepared a speech to share at the funeral mass and discussed it with our brother. Well our brother decided that what he had to share was more important, so he never called Jimmy up to share what he had written. Jimmy was heartbroken, and we all were too because we knew how much it meant to him.

Not even a week after dad's funeral, my brother called me to tell me that he decided not to use my law firm to process dad's estate in Probate Court, but rather he wanted to use another local attorney, whom everyone in the legal field knew was one of the biggest schiesters in the City. When I questioned my brother as to why all the sudden my boss, Attorney Crean, would be out of the picture after serving dad all the previous years, he said he didn't like him. Attorney Crean had prepared dad's Last Will and Testament, and dad trusted him. My brother knew that dad had appointed him Executor of his Will, so he said he was in charge and was going to use another attorney because Attorney Crean did not represent him well during his divorce. I kept asking my brother where all this was coming from, and he kept saying that he trusted this other attorney more. What a joke. I knew this other attorney for years, and he had a reputation for representing criminals and for running a very shady law practice. As soon as I hung up the phone with my brother, I called Attorney Crean to let him know that he would not be handling the probate estate of my father, and I apologized that my brother had decided to use the other attorney. Mr. Crean said he was not surprised and before he hung up he told me to check dad's real estate on the Land Records. When I questioned why I needed to do that, Mr. Crean told me to just check the Land Records.

After being a legal secretary for over 20 years, I was able to check the title of real estate on the Land Records. So later that day, I went to the Town Clerk's Office and asked permission to check the land records for my dad's real estate. Well, I was sickened to find a Quit Claim Deed from my dad to my brother dated February 25, 2000, (the date of dad's surgery) signed and witnessed in Waterbury, Connecticut!!! It was obvious that my brother had signed dad's name on the deed, which deed relinquished dad's life use to my brother, free and clear. This meant that the family home was in my brother's name only and he was the sole owner of the real estate and dad had no legal right to the property. I went home and immediately called the attorney who signed and notarized the fraudulent deed, and spoke with his secretary. When I told the secretary that my dad could not have been in Waterbury, CT on February 25, 2000 because he was undergoing a quadruple by-pass operation in New Haven, CT and further that dad's signature was forged by my brother, she put me on hold and had the attorney pick up. When I explained to the attorney the severity of the fraudulent deed and the unlawful notarizing that he had done, the attorney became very belligerent and told me that I did not know what I was talking about, that he met with my dad and my brother on that day and told me I didn't have any right to question him. I informed the attorney that I would be filing a grievance against him with the State of Connecticut because of his unlawful actions, and he abruptly hung up on me.

It so happened that my brother had called each of us to come to "his house" and get what we wanted, because he was only going to make this offer once. So my sister, Janice, my friend, Patti, my three little children and me went up to our family home for the last time. I brought the deed that I found on the Land Records with me because I was going to confront my brother on it. Now I knew why he wanted to use a different attorney to handle the estate, and I wanted to see how he was going to explain how this deed ever got signed and filed on the Land Records.

While we looked around to see what, if anything we wanted from the house, my brother came into the kitchen to ask us if we were done. I decided to confront my brother about the deed that I found on the Land Records. I had my purse in my dad's bedroom off the kitchen, so I walked in and took out the deed and I told my brother that I found the deed he fraudulently signed. My brother ran across the kitchen and put his fist right up against my left cheek, and screamed that he had had enough of my crap. I told him that he couldn't bully his way around everyone anymore. He turned and walked away grumbling and I picked up the kitchen chair to hit him with, but my sister grabbed it and told me not to stoop to his level. I began screaming that

I was on to him and all his schemes. I told him that I now figured out that the appointment that he couldn't cancel the day we were having dad's funeral was his mortgage closing. Now he really freaks out and yells that he ended up changing the date of his mortgage closing on dad's house and realized that he just admitted to trying to get all the equity in the family home. I told him that he would not get away with it, that I was going to file a grievance against the attorney that notarized the deed, and that we were going to ask the Probate judge to remove him from being Executor of dad's Will. My brother then said that he was good friends with the Probate judge, and he wasn't worried about anything. I told my brother that he better get ready for a fight, grabbed my children and left.

In the following weeks, I filed my grievance with the State against the attorney who prepared and notarized the deed. When the date for the hearing on dad's estate came to Probate Court all my siblings and their spouses, except for our sister, Phyllis, who lived in Nebraska with her husband and boys, appeared at the Probate Court hearing to contest the appointment of Executor. Our next oldest sibling, Daniel, was named as the Alternate Executor in dad's Last Will and Testament, however, Probate Judge James Lawlor, decided he would appoint a neutral person of his choosing to act in the capacity of Executor. Judge Lawlor also advised my family that he would only allow us to speak through an attorney, and therefore, we were instructed to hire an attorney to represent us at future probate hearings.

We hired an attorney and we were informed that our brother fired his attorney and was now being represented by another attorney. We were further advised that Judge Lawlor had appointed Attorney Michael Conway to be the Executor of dad's Will. Red flags immediately went up for me. Attorney Sullivan was the son of another Judge, who just happened to be very friendly with Judge Lawlor. Attorney Conway was as associate of Attorney Sullivan. Now I realized that everyone was on the take, and that our brother was definitely up to no good.

To make a very long and sad story short, it took almost two years to settle dad's estate. I did grieve the attorney who prepared, signed and notarized the fraudulent deed. The worst that could have happened to him was that he could have been disbarred. The grievance committee decided that because he was a new, young lawyer he was inexperienced and did not have adequate supervision at the law firm he was working for, so he was not disbarred, but reprimanded for his wrongful acts. I ended up filing a grievance against Judge James Lawlor because he would not allow us to review all portions of dad's probate file and because he allowed our brother to sell off dad's personal belongings, his automobile and his house without any involvement of our family whatsoever. The State of Connecticut Judicial Grievance Committee did not find any wrong doing against Judge Lawlor because the committee stated that I did not cite the correct State Statute in my grievance against the Judge. They did reprimand Judge Lawlor not allowing us to review dad's entire file and we were told to go to Probate Court and review the entire file.

This whole experience with my brother and the legal system strongly enhanced my desire to stand up for what's right and stand against wrong doers. Everyone told me I was wasting my time to grieve the attorney and the Judge, but DON'T TELL ME I CAN'T. The only reason why people don't do something is because of fear of failure, fear of man or fear of what others may think. The lawyer didn't get disbarred and the Judge wasn't found guilty, but the grievances stay in their State records and remain there as something that they may need to provide an explanation for when they need to purchase malpractice insurance. I believe in my heart that the attorney would never repeat that mistake again and learned from his mistake. As for Judge Lawlor, he smugly believes he was right and did nothing illegal.

Bottom line, if you are in a situation where you believe someone in authority has done or is doing something illegal, please don't just let it go. There are avenues that you can take to defend yourself or your family. God would want you to stand up for what is right, and He will give you the strength and confidence to do what you need to do.

CHAPTER 9

I can't believe I did it. I began my life as a stay home mom in September 1991 and there I was FINALLY through taking care of babies. I think I had to tell myself a thousand times over the last 10 years that "I can do this". Being a stay home mom is, without a doubt, one of the hardest jobs there is.

All three kids were in school all day, and I went back to work at the law firm from 10:00 to 2:00 Monday through Friday. My oldest child, Christina, was in fourth grade, Alaina was in first and Zachary was in kindergarten. Many of Christina's friends were leaving the public school they were attending and enrolling in the local Catholic Schools. Many parents were worried that if they waited until their child was in fifth grade to change schools, there wouldn't be enough room. The problem was that the middle schools in Waterbury were so bad that police officers were assigned to monitor daily activity. Christina was in an accelerated program which allowed her to go the middle school on Mondays and participate in a sixth grade class. The middle school in our district was a very low income, urban school. Christina liked the opportunity to go to sixth grade classes one day a week, but she hated the school. The middle school she was going to was the middle school she would have to go to when she finished fifth grade, and she begged us not to send her there. We were now faced with a dilemma of enrolling Christina in a private school and pay tuition or think about moving out of Waterbury. At the time the mill rate was going up to 90 percent or more, and we knew our house and car taxes were going go way up.

So we decided to put the house on the market in February of 2001. We didn't hire a real estate agent, we just put a "For Sale" sign in front of our house and put an ad in our local newspaper. While our house was on the market, we began our search for a home in the surrounding towns. We wanted a home with four bedrooms so each of our children could have their own room and two baths. We had a private back yard in the house we were selling, so we also wanted a private back yard. We knew what we could afford and we prayed to God to help us find the exact house.

We had buyers for our house within three months, however, we still did not find a new home for our family. The buyers had cash to buy our home, so the closing was scheduled for early May, 2001. Since we did not have a house to move into, we agreed to rent back our home from the new owners. Our real estate agent kept pushing a new construction home in Wolcott, but we didn't like the style of house the builders were planning to put on the lot. Jim found a house online and we went to look at it. It was exactly what we were looking for, but there was already a deposit on it. Our agent was familiar with the house and knew that it had been built by the same builders offering the new construction that she was pushing us for. We told our agent that if she could get the builders to put that same house on the lot in questions, then we would have a deal. Well, guess what?? The builders agreed and we entered into a construction contract.

Shortly after signing the contract for the new construction, Jim got laid off. Now we had to find a mortgage company to give us a mortgage based on my part time income. Because our credit score was high, the mortgage company agreed to give us a mortgage in my name only. Attorney Crean was handling our closings and he was very nervous that we were going to end up over our heads. Jim met with Attorney Crean one day and explained to him that he had been laid off before and God always provided a job for him, and that we were going forward with the closing because we trust God.

We moved into our new home in November, 2001. We couldn't afford to have the builders finish the lower level, so Jim framed out and finished Alaina's bedroom and our family room. Jim had everything done within a few months, and we settled into our new home, new school and new town.

When all my children were in school full time, I went back to work in the office from 10:00 a.m. to 2:00 p.m., so I would be able to see them off to school and to be home for them when they got off the bus. I still worked a couple of nights a week, so I could keep that door open if any one of my children were sick and I needed to stay home.

It was nice to be back in the office again, and to see all my co-workers, who were really more like friends to me. In the ten years or so while I was a stay home mom, our errand girl, Karen, graduated law school and became a partner in our firm. It was a little crazy to see this young girl that used to run all our errands working in the firm as a boss. I was in my early 40's by then and I realized that I have been a legal secretary in the firm for over 20 years and that I was going to be there for another 20 before I retired. That thought scared me. I just couldn't see myself working in the law firm for another 20 years. The pay was not very good, however, the hours were flexible, so that was one reason why I stayed put. But the final straw came one day in early 2005. It was early in the day and I was making copies at the copier and another secretary was at the counter filing and I began a conversation with her. The former errand girl, now partner was in her office around the corner and came out with her hands on her hips and asked me if I was keeping Deborah from her work. I told her that we were both still working, so I was not keeping her from her work. Let me back up here, the law firm we worked at had very strict rules. There was to be no talking while you worked, no personal phone calls, no radio playing, etc. We all obeyed these rules to a point, but it is actually impossible for a bunch of women to not have a conversation at some time during the day. Working there could be very stressful at times, and many times we just needed to talk and laugh for a few minutes to break the stressful mood.

Anyway, Karen is standing there with her hands on her hips and demanding answers as to why we were talking during work time. I just shrugged, shook my head and quietly finished making my copies. A few hours later, I was at the copier again and another secretary, Terri, came into the main office and heard Deborah talking on the phone. Terri, being the buster that she is, says to me, "Is that Deborah on a personal call?" I said, "Yeah, and it's not me keeping her from her work this time!" As soon as I said that, Karen called out to me from her office to get in there right now.

My first thought when I heard her call me into her office was she cannot be serious. She was taking her position way too serious. I entered her office and Karen was standing at her desk with her hands on her hips and she says, "Are you mocking me?" I turned around and shut the door and told her that if she thinks that I am going to work another 20 years under the same conditions as we did when she was our errand girl that she was crazy. I reminded her of how much she disliked how the office was run and here she is now getting all bent out of shape. I told her that I could not work under these conditions in such a tense atmosphere and strict rules. I told her she turned into the exact person that she used to despise and with that, I walked out. A few minutes later, the head attorney in the firm asked me to go into the conference room. When I entered, Karen was sitting at the conference table, sobbing into a tissue and I was motioned to take a seat.

Now I have the head attorney of the firm telling me how I owe Karen an apology, that I after all that he did for me by allowing me to work nights all these years that I owe him an apology as well. At this point, I looked him in the eye and told him that it was I whom he should be thanking for cranking out all kinds of work every night, work that no one else wanted to do. I reminded him of how I worked nights as a temporary worker with no benefits, no paid holidays or sick time. I then told him that the office was a very "sucky" place to work and I could not work another 20 years under the watchful eye of Karen. Then Karen puts the icing on the cake by telling me that she had instructed Deborah before I came back to working days that she should no talk to me when and if I would start a conversation in the office during working hours! Now, I realize that she set me up and was just waiting for the time to come for me to talk to Deborah. Really, now I'm really upset and told her that I was extremely upset with Deborah that she would agree to such a thing and secondly that she was going to take over the office worse than her predecessor. When the meeting was over, I went back to work knowing that I had to get out of there as soon as I could.

When I got home I discussed everything with Jim and he agreed I needed to get out of there. The big question was where to go. Should I apply to other law firms? Should I possibly go back to school? Should I just look into a whole new profession? In the weeks that followed, I prayed and asked God where He could use me. I shared the Lord with all my co-workers over the years. I prayed with some clients that allowed me to. However, I wanted more out of my life. I wanted a job where I could do something that would allow me to minister to people. I really didn't want to be locked into another office job where you put your nose to the grindstone and maybe once in a while get to do something that would have eternal value.

I was looking at any and all jobs related to law. Judicial Marshall? Constable? Corrections Officer? I just wanted a job that would put me around different people that needed someone to encourage them with promises of God. As I began researching the requirements for these various jobs, I noticed that the requirements for Corrections Officer where very similar to a Police Officer. A couple of weeks after I really started looking into being a Corrections Officer, there was an article in the newspaper that the Town of Wolcott was looking to hire new officers. I immediately showed Jim the article and asked him what he thought. I explained that the first thing to do was apply and take a written test. After the written test, I would have to pass a physical agility test which included sit ups, bench pressing half my body weight, sit and reach and running a mile and a half in 15 minutes. Jim agreed that my law experience would probably make it easy for me to pass the written test. I also was and had been faithful in exercising and keeping in shape, so we both felt I could do the physical test as well. So, I applied for the job.

I took the written test and knew I did well. I soon received a letter congratulating me and a date for me to take the physical test. I started running the high school track soon after I applied and got me time to where it had to be. Here I was 45 years old, competing against all these 21+ year old males and females. I prayed and asked God to give me the strength and ability to pass the physical test, and I prayed that if I did not pass, then I would take that as a sign that being an officer was not part of God's plan for my life. Well, I did it!! I passed all four stations and got my CHIP card. A few weeks later, I received a call to come to the Wolcott Police Station for an interview. I was excited and yet nervous, but I was trusting God all the way. The interview was with a couple of Police Chiefs from neighboring towns and a Captain from the Wolcott Police Department. The Captain greeted me in the lobby and brought me to the interviewing room. He was cold as cold could be to me. As we were walking down the hallway to the interview room, he says "So you want to be a cop, huh?" as he looked down at all 5 foot of me. By the end of the interview, I just knew that the Captain did not like me or want me in the department. I went home and told my husband that I was not going to be picked for the job. I was upset, but I had other applications filed in different towns, and I was determined not to give up.

A couple of weeks later, I read in the paper that Wolcott hired two new police officers. One was the captain's relative and the other was another officer's relative. Everyone said that it was who you knew in the small Towns, so I didn't let it discourage me. While waiting on Wolcott, I had taken tests in two other cities and was keeping my physical skills up.

During this time, I continued to work at the law firm and never told anyone that I had begun to look for a new career. One day my co-worker, Margie, told me about a job that her son had at a girls' lock down facility. He was working at a branch in Litchfield, but the branch in Waterbury was looking for help. The place was called Stepping Stone and it was a facility which had teenage girls who had been arrested for different crimes. The facility was a locked down facility which the girls had been sent to by the Court in an effort to rehabilitate them so they would not have to serve time in a women's prison. She knew how unhappy I was at the office and suggested that I go check it out. So I figured I would contact them for an interview and see what it was all about. I had made up my mind that I was going to try to become a police officer and I knew it was going to take time, so I would rather at least work in a facility where I liked my job, rather than stay at the office much longer.

I few weeks later, I had my interview at Stepping Stone. The director explained to me that the opening was for third shift, that as a staff member, I would be responsible for monitoring the girls in my assigned wing and make sure they didn't try to escape, harm themselves or each other. The pay rate was $5.00 less per hour that what I was making, but I would be working full time, rather than part time. I explained to the Director that I was in the process of applying to different cities and towns to be a police officer, and that if I were to succeed, then I would have to leave. The Director didn't seem to mind that and told me that if I wanted the job, it was mine. Wow. I didn't expect that so quickly. I told her that I would need to talk to my husband and see if we could work around the hours with our three children having to get off to school in the morning. At the time my children were 14, 11 and 10. They were able to get themselves ready for school, but we wanted to be sure one of us would be home to see them get on the bus safe and sound.

Jim and I discussed it, and we agreed we would be able to do the schedule. I would make it home at 7:15 a.m. and he left at 7:00 a.m. the bus came at 7:35 a.m. After the children left for school, I would go to sleep until they got home around 2:00 p.m. I called the Director back a couple of days later and told her that I was going to take the job, but I had to give my two week notice to the office. The following Monday, I went in to the boss and told him that I found another job and that I was giving him my notice. All he did was look up from his desk and say "Okay". That was it. I worked there 25 years and that was all he said. I got up, left his office and made my announcement to my co-workers. They were all surprised that the boss didn't ask me to stay or offer me more money to stay, but I told them that he knew how unhappy I was there and he probably was expecting me to come in sooner or later. It was hard to say goodbye to my friends that I have known for so many years, but the time for change had come.

CHAPTER 10

I'M STILL PINCHING MYSELF THAT I actually left the law firm. I was excited to see what God had in store for me at the new job. I knew I would be meeting young girls who probably never had anyone share the love of Christ with them and I was happy that I would be able to make a difference in someone's life. Shortly before starting at Stepping Stone I took the police test for the City of Waterbury and I was honest with the Director before I took the job that I was trying to apply for a police officer position in various towns, and that if I were to actually get hired, I would give them plenty of notice. The Director did not seem to mind, maybe because she thought it would never happen or maybe she felt I was a good fit for their facility.

I had training outside the facility the first week. We were taught how to take down the girls safely, without hurting them ourselves. They explained that all staff was responsible for the wing they were assigned to. We were given two-way radios to communicate with each other. Two staff members were assigned to each wing. My first night or two I worked with my supervisor, Kim. Kim was very helpful in explaining what had to be done and how what to do in case one or two of the girls were to act up.

The hardest part of the job in the first week or so was staying up all night. Falling asleep on the job was the not allowed and could get you fired. I had to train myself to sleep during the day while my kids were at school. The weekends were the hardest because everyone was usually home making noise. However, I got into the groove of it and I began to adjust.

As staff, we were encouraged to read the files of the girls that were in the home. Many, almost all, of the girls had been sexually assaulted by their mother's boyfriend or a relative. Many were left alone to care for younger siblings and most were made to feel that they were not wanted or loved. Once I read the girls files, I saw them in a different light. I had two teenage girls myself, and I know how difficult it can be to raise them. I couldn't imagine that one of the girls could be my daughter and as their mom not love and protect them like a real mom would.

I tried not to let their bad attitudes and sassy mouths get to me. I knew they were all hurting, each in their own way, and they each were lashing out at everyone because they were so hurt and rejected. Part of third shift's job was to clean the lavatories and common areas. It was good, in a way, because doing the chores kept me busy and awake. We did mandatory bed checks every 10-15 minutes and had to give an account over the radio whether or not the girls were all sleeping, if one or two were awake, etc.

In my first few weeks there I was paired with another staff member, Ruthy. She was much younger than me, a single mom with a little boy. Ruthy and I spent many many nights talking about our lives. We soon realized that we were very much alike. Her mom treated her other siblings nice, but was mean to her. My dad had done the same to me with my two sisters. We talked about how unfair it was and how much pain it caused us and we related that pain to the pain the girls in the house must have. We both felt the same way that we were there to try to make a difference in their lives.

A few months after I started working at Stepping Stone, a notice was posted that they needed more Med-Certs on each shift. The Med-Certs were trained how to give medications to the girls in the house. Many of the girls were on narcotics, and each pill had to be accounted for. Ruthy and I decided to take the class and I ended up becoming a Med-Cert on the third shift. In addition to giving the girls their medication, the Med-Certs were called to check on any girl in the house who may be sick during the night. Each girl's medical chart listed what we could give them for headaches, cramps, nausea, etc. It was after becoming Med-Cert that I truly began to love the girls. If one of them was nauseous, I would do what I would do for my own child. I would make them a cup of tea and some dry toast. One night one of the girls was sick to her stomach and after I brought her some crackers and gingerale, she asked me why I was being so nice to her. When I questioned her, she told me none of the other Med-Certs ever did that. I explained to her that I had three children of my own and that I was going to treat them like I would my own. When other Med-Certs learned that I went a little beyond what they did, they gave me a hard time. Most of the other staff were young, single people who were going to college and just working to pay bills. I knew where they were coming from, but I felt as long as my supervisors were okay with what I was doing, I was going to continue.

Another girl that really touched my heart was this very large, mean, argumentative and difficult young girl. I was called to her bed during the night because she was not feeling well. When I got to her room, she was burning up with fever and had the chills. I got a blanket and a cold face cloth and sat with her. Once she cooled down I gave her some crackers and gingerale and she fell asleep. In the morning, she was one of the first ones up and when I went to put the light on in her room she called me over and whispered to me, "Miss thank you for taking care of me last night. No one has ever done that for me before." I held back my tears and gave her a hug and told her that I was glad she was feeling better. When I got off work that morning, I couldn't stop thinking about what she said. How could someone be 15 years old and never remember someone doing something as simple as that for her?

Many times I would tell my children how these girls were raised and how fortunate they were that they had a mom and dad and aunts and uncles that loved them. How lucky they were to have their own room in a nice home, in a nice neighborhood. I just wanted my children to be grateful for what they have and to thank God each day. Not only that, but to also pray for the hundreds of girls and boys who do not have a normal family life. It was and is important to me to always be aware that there are many people less fortunate than us. I tried to instill into my children to be thankful for what they had, not always wanting more and more things, but to find joy and happiness within. My children were raised in the church, they were taught Christian values and I prayed that they would keep their hearts after God.

The most difficult part of my job at Stepping Stone was the mandatory stay overs. Each one of us on shift we were forced to stay over if someone called out on first shift. There was a rotating system, so we all took turns, but it was very difficult to work another eight hours and then try to go home and rest and come back at 11:00. During the nice weather, we had to stay over once in a while. When winter came, that's when all hell broke loose. Many times one by one everyone on first shift would start calling out because of snow, not calling to say they would be a couple of hours late, so we would only have to stay until they got there. One night the entire first shift, except for two staff members, called out. I couldn't imagine that the Director didn't have any rules in place about preparing for storms. Imagine calling out every time it snowed. My husband worked 40 minutes from home and he would get up an hour early just to clear the driveway. After about the fourth snowstorm, I made an appointment to speak to the Director about how lax the first shift staff was about coming in during a snow storm. She agreed with me and said she would look into it.

I did enjoy working at Stepping Stone, all in all. I really felt that God opened many opportunities for me share His love with the girls. Many times the girls would ask me why I would want to work at a place like Stepping Stone and with all the girls and their problems. I would tell them that I didn't think badly of any of the girls there, that I they all had very difficult lives and I encouraged them that they could do anything with their lives if they set their minds to it.

Throughout the months that I was working at Stepping Stone, I was involved in the hiring process of the City of Waterbury for a job at their Police Department. I had interviews, physical agility tests, lie detector test, psychological test and medical examination. A short time before my year anniversary at Stepping Stone, I received word that I was accepted into the Waterbury Police Academy. I met with the director and gave her my two week notice. She was happy for me, but informed me that she and the administration had just met and were going to promote me to Supervisor. I explained that I would have definitely accepted the new position, however, my heart was to be a police officer. The director asked me to let the girls know that I was leaving, as she knew that I had become close to many of them. It was very difficult for me to tell the girls. Many of them asked me if they were the reason why I was leaving, if I could come back and visit. I told them I had no idea how the Police Academy was, how much time it would consume, but I would always think of them and pray for them. Sad to say, aside from Ruthy, there were no staff members that I said anything to.

CHAPTER 11

IT WAS REALLY HAPPENING. I was purchasing my police recruit uniforms and getting ready for the first day of the academy and orientation. Classes were to start on Thursday, April 21, 2006 and on Monday, April 18th, I received a call from Human Resources that I did not pass my eye exam and would not be able to start on Wednesday, unless I could get laser surgery on my eyes before then. I was in shock and asked them how did I NOT PASS my eye exam, which was a month ago? The woman explained that my vision without correction was too poor to be a police officer. WHAT???? Are you kidding me?? I immediately called the Lieutenant in charge of the academy and asked him what was going on, and he just said if Human Resources said that then you're out. I was so upset and confused that I got in my car and went to the medical facility that the City sent me to for my medical examination and asked to speak to someone who was in charge. I spoke to the Supervisor and she took me to her office and showed me some form from the State which requires police officers to have certain vision, without correction. I asked her why was I not told this immediately when they did my eye exam?? It wasn't the kind of exam where the results came later. She said all results were sent to Human Resources immediately after each recruit had their exam and that's all she knew. So now Human Resources supposedly had my results for one month, but waited two days before I was to start the academy to tell me this?? When I got home I called Human Resources to speak to whomever was in charge of the medical examination results and was told that the woman was out of the office, but they would leave her a message.

I called my husband and discussed with him if we could afford laser surgery and if I should even get it. He suggested I call our eye doctor to see what she thought. Our eye doctor was also a person who went to church with us and when I called her she told me to go to her office right away so she could do a test on my eyes to see if laser would be an option or not. I went to her office the next morning for the test and found out that I would be able to have laser on my eyes. I called Human Resources again to speak to the woman in charge and was told that she was out of the office again. I explained to the woman that I would be willing to have laser surgery to correct my vision, but she told me only the Supervisor could make a decision to reinstate me.

I was so frustrated and confused. I had prayed for God to open the doors for me to become a police officer and all along the doors were opened. I was able to pass all the tests and to come down to the wire and have it all be for nothing, just didn't make any sense. Our orientation was to be on Wednesday evening and I was not going to be able to attend with the rest of the class. I wasn't sure what or where to turn. I had already quit Stepping Stone and if I didn't get into the academy I would not have a job. The way it works with the City is that you receive the base pay a police officer received, along with benefits while in the academy.

Hardest thing I had to do next was to call the director at Stepping Stone and ask for my job back. She was happy to have me back, however, I lost all seniority and would not have weekends off anymore. I thanked the director and agreed that the following Monday I would go back to third shift. I was so depressed and confused I could hardly pray. I called and left messages two or three times on Tuesday and Wednesday, still no response. I really believed I heard from God that evening when He reminded me of the scripture in Jeremiah 29:11 "I know the plans I have for you declares the Lord, not to harm you but to give you hope for the future". I trusted God that He did have a plan for me, that this situation did not take Him by surprise, that He would work it all for good. BUT HOW??

On Thursday I tried to call Human Resources again, no luck. I was finally told that the woman was out of the office all week giving Fire Department exams, but would be back tomorrow morning. I asked if she could call me first thing tomorrow, and I was assured that she would. Friday morning I waited until 9:00 a.m. and called Human Resources. The woman was in and actually took my call. She quickly informed me that she had my many messages, and was going to call me. I asked her how did she NOT have the results of my eye examination when they were done in early March. She informed me that Concentra, the medical office did not send them until very recently. I explained to her that I had checked with my eye doctor and I would be able to have laser surgery. I asked her if I were to have laser surgery would she promise me a seat in the next academy class. She indicated that she was not in the position to make that promise to me. Now I am furious. I ask her how can she be the one who decides that I would not be able to be in the current class, but not be able to promise me a seat in the next class. She took the position that she only goes by the results of the medical office. I explained to her that the City of Waterbury hired Concentra to do their medical exams and they are an agent for the City and if Concentra was not capable of performing their duties in a timely manner, it falls back on the City. I further told her that I was not going to take this sitting down, that I was going to consult with a lawyer about my rights and the liability of the City. She basically told me to do what I had to do and hung up.

I called a litigation attorney that I knew from my years as a legal secretary and he recommend a good labor law attorney. I contacted the attorney and was instructed to send him an email of all the details and circumstances regarding my case. I no sooner hung up the phone when the woman from Human Resources called me to inform me that she spoke to someone in the Police Department and that if I agreed to have laser surgery by July 1st, then I would be able to be in the present academy class. I agreed that I would have laser surgery by July 1st and she told me to get to the academy by noon.

The Waterbury Police Academy was located in downtown Waterbury. I was instructed to report to Lt. Sherman McGrew when I arrived. I was excited and nervous at the same time, but I quickly changed into some sweats, as instructed, and reported to Lt. McGrew's office at 11:45. Upon my arrival, Lt. McGrew informed me that I had to redo my physical agility test. He brought me to the fitness room in the academy where I did my 30 sit-ups in one minute, benched half my body weight one full repetition and did my sit and reach agility. I passed those tests and was told that I needed to repeat my mile and a half run. I met the lieutenant at the designated test run sight, and did my run in less than the 15 minute time requirement. Lt. McGrew advised me that I needed to get back to the academy before class resumed at 1300 hours. Lt. McGrew further advised me that every recruit is only allowed to miss four days of class, and that I had already missed one and a half days. He reminded that I had to have my laser surgery before July 1st and advised me to make sure I would be able to return to class. I was getting the very distinct feeling that he was not happy to have me in class and that he was giving me the heads up that he was not going to be giving me any breaks. I assured Lt. McGrew that I would be sure to schedule my surgery on a Friday, as to not miss that much time from class.

When we returned to the academy, everyone had returned from their lunch break and were waiting for the instructor to begin class. Lt. McGrew brought me in front of the class and introduced me. He asked that one of my fellow recruits offer to lend me a set of physical fitness clothes until mine come in. Everyone just sat there and steered at me, and I looked back at this room filled with mostly young men and women in their early 20s I felt so old and awkward, but I knew in my heart that God had opened these doors for me and I was going to do this.

I was showed where my seat in class would be. We were seated in alpha-betical order and our seats rotated one chair to the right every week. No sooner did I settle down in my seat, a female recruit, Nadine, introduced herself to me, welcomed me to the class and told me that she had an extra physical fitness outfit that I could borrow until mine came in. She blessed me so much, and I was very relieved that I would have the proper attire. She told me to meet her at the police station after class and she would give me a pair of shorts and t-shirt to wear on Monday.

Just before class ended at 1600 hours, Lt. McGrew addressed the class and explained to us what we were to expect in the coming weeks. We were to do our morning runs on Mondays, Wednesdays and Fridays. We began the first week running a half mile, and we were informed that every week (the academy was 26 weeks) we would add a half mile to our run until we reached 10 miles! On Tuesdays and Thursdays our PT (physical fitness routine) would be to run the staircases in the adjoining ramp garage and we would add additional flights each week until we finished running 110 flights of stairs, in honor of those who lost their lives in 911 World Trade Center attacks. Lt. McGrew reminded us "children" to stay out of trouble over the weekend and to remember that we represented the Waterbury Police Department. The class responded with a resounding "Yes Sir".

CHAPTER 12

THE POLICE ACADEMY IS RUN paramilitary, we were to salute all department heads whenever we were in their presence. We operated on military time. Lt. McGrew had a strong military background, and was still active in the military. Lt. McGrew would have anyone one of us, or the whole class, drop and give him 20 pushups, if one of us did something out of line or unacceptable. A few of the males in our class were straight from the military, having come back from serving time in Iraq and Afganastan. Many times Lt. McGrew would call out one of them to lead the class.

I was excited when Monday morning came, so I could officially be one of the recruits in the class. Each week Lt. McGrew would appoint one of us to be the class head. This person would lead the class in our warm up exercises before our PT each day. We did cadence during our runs to keep time. Lt. McGrew had already had started giving some of the recruits a nicknames, which would be the name that he would call us. Only a couple of us had names on my first day, which my fellow classmates filled me in on. My plan was to keep as quiet as possible and stay under the radar.

Our run was one mile that Monday. We ran a mile through town and ended up at the Police Station, where we each were assigned a locker to keep our uniforms in. We would run to the station and had a short time to freshen up and change into our uniforms. The run wasn't that bad for me until the final stretch to the station, which was on a slight hill. I started to run out of steam and was struggling to keep up. When we were in front of the station, we would get in formation before we would file in to the station. As I was panting, Lt. McGrew comes face to face with me and says, "Robinson you seem a bit winded, you gonna make it?". I responded, "Yes Sir". Lt. McGrew then goes on to say that he read my bio and I stated in there that I was in excellent physical condition. Lt. McGrew then asks me if I ever saw the movie Rainman, because the character in that movie would always say, "I'm an excellent driver". I responded that I had not seen the movie. Lt. McGrew then informed me that my moniker from now on was going to be Rainman. And so it was, I was now Rainman.

After a couple of weeks there were many of us with new names, Paddywagon, Skippy, Red, Mr. Ed and Scantron – to name a few. Our days in the academy were always full with very little down time. We had various members of the Waterbury Police Department teaching us about motor vehicle laws, domestic violence, ethnic law, DUI training, Emergency Response Training and drug and alcohol abuse, just to name a few. As interesting as the classes were, many times we all had to fight to keep awake, especially when we began running the five mile plus runs!

In April 2006 when the academy class started, the movie the Passion of the Christ movie was out in the theaters. The movie was very moving and had a huge impact on my life. The torture that Jesus took for us was beyond anyone's ability to bear, yet he did not give in to his pain and suffering. Many, many times when the runs were longer and we had to wear our duty belt with our radio, baton, handcuffs, pepper spray and firearm, I would remember the scenes from the movie and pray for Jesus to give me His strength to endure. The runs were hard enough, now running with all the extra weight on our waists was ever more difficult. I am certain that Jesus did give me the strength to run those miles every week.

I had my laser eye surgery the first Friday in July. Thank God everything went well. I had to get epi-Lasik, which the eye surgeon suggested was safer for police officers, athletes and others whose job could entail getting an eye injury. The simple Lasik procedure is when the doctor cuts your cornea in a pie shape and opens the cornea to do the laser surgery. The cornea remains weak after that kind of procedure, so if one were to get hit in the eye a corneal tear could occur much easily. Therefore, it was suggested that I have

Epi-Lasik, where the doctor removes the cornea to do the laser surgery. The cornea grows back in less than a week, however, your eyes are extremely sensitive to light. Because I could not take too much time off for my eye surgery, I had the surgery late in the day on a Friday, allowing me to only miss a half a day in class. I needed to heal over the weekend and the following Monday, which put me out of class for a total of 3 days.

When I returned to class the following Tuesday after my laser surgery, I had to get "permission" to be "out of uniform" to wear sunglasses during the runs. Lt. McGrew initially made a big deal out of it, but I was allowed to wear sunglasses for the remainder of the academy for all outside activites.

My two favorite aspects of the academy were going to the range to learn how to use our firearm and defensive tactics. We also had to get tased and pepper sprayed, so that we could understand fully how these two less lethal weapons were used and how they affected you. Before our class got tased, we heard all sorts of horror stories from other officers. Sometimes after being tased you will involuntary urinate, so one of our classmates brought in a box of Depends! I was bracing myself for the five seconds of extreme pain by comparing it to labor pain, which lasts much, much longer than five seconds. In my mind, I could stand five seconds. There were about seven females in our class and I have to admit all the females took the taser much better than our male classmates. When the taser is shot, it releases two cords that carry the current and at the end are something like a fish hook, so when it is shot, the hook does not easily some out, in case the person needs to receive another five minute shot. Probably the worst part of the taser was pulling the hooks out of our skin.

When our class was scheduled for the pepper spray, it was only a month after my laser surgery, so I couldn't get pepper sprayed with my class. However, being peppered sprayed is 100% worse than getting tased. The pepper spray is an oily, gritty pepper mixture that is extremely difficult to wash out of your eyes and off your skin. After we were sprayed, we had to fight off each other and handcuff them, which forces you to keep your eyes open. The reason for this is because many times when we pepper spray a suspect the wind may blow some of the spray back in your face and they had to have us experience the feeling of being sprayed and also of having to continue to get the suspect into custody. Once we have completed that, we were led to another area where someone filled both our hands with Dawn dish soap and we put that directly into our eyes and on our skin. Then there were buckets of water that we splashed and splashed our faces and neck with until we could at least open our eyes. The pepper spray has to be patted off, not rubbed off because it will be rubbed in, which is worse. The effect of the pepper spray lasts for hours and hours, and sometimes days on some people.

Even though being tased and pepper sprayed was not fun, it was the most hilarious times because it was so funny to watch each other's reaction. Also, it was very important that we all experienced the pain of both, so that if we ever had to testify in Court about the effect of either of those two less lethal weapons, we could say exactly how we felt and exactly what we were able to do and not due. We also had to do a driving course where we learned how to get out of a skid, back up through tight areas and drive under stressful conditions. This course was also very important to experience because in the real world when we are going lights and sirens, we need to be able to keep our vehicle under control and safe.

As the weeks went on in the academy we were given duty belts to wear each day. Little by little all of the gear we needed to carry on our duty belts was added. Our handcuffs, a rubber firearm, extra magazines, taser, baton and a pouch for latex gloves. We still had to continue our runs throughout the City, an extra half mile was added each week until we reached our maximum of a 10 mile run with a full duty belt! Not only did we do the run Monday, Wednesday and Friday mornings, we ran flights of stairs in the nearby ramp garage on Tuesday and Thursday mornings. We started with a few flights and we finished with running 110 flights of stairs in honor of those who climbed the two Twin Towers on 9/11. Also on Tuesdays and Thursdays, we had to do chin ups with our duty belts on. Because I am so short, I always had to have one of the guys give me a boost up on the bar and so I could do my chin ups. Our lieutenant wanted us to try and do 10 and it took everything I had to get those 10 done.

Our most difficult runs were during the summer months, as we had the heat to battle as well. Throughout the months, various recruits had to be excused from both runs because of injuries. I thank God I was able to complete every run. There were many days that my legs and back were so sore that I just wanted to ask permission to miss PT, but I never wanted anyone to think it was because of my age that I wasn't able to keep up.

Before we knew it, we had completed our 26 weeks in the police academy and it was graduation night. My husband, three children and many family and friends were in the audience at the Palace Theater to cheer on our graduating class. Our class had prepared a video of various special moments from the academy, which was awesome.

Me and my beautiful girls from the law firm.

Graduating Class of 2006

Me, my husband and my three beautiful children.

At the end of the ceremony we were all talking and taking pictures with our families and friends. Lt. McGrew came up to me and in his usual serious tone says, "Officer Robinson, how old are you?" "Forty-eight, Sir" I replied. "Come with me Officer Robinson, I want to introduce you to someone" he said. I looked at my husband and family and all I could think of was "who was this guy going to introduce me to". Well, Lt. McGrew brings me over to the Chief of Police, Neil O'Leary. Lt. McGrew introduces me to the Chief telling him who I was, how old I was, how I had laser surgery, how I never missed a run, never backed down, etc. etc. I looked at Lt. McGrew and he had this big smile on his face. I shook the Chief's hand and told him that I was very grateful to be a part of the Waterbury Police Department. Lt. McGrew gave me a pat on the back and said "good job recruit Robinson". So, the old tough guy was really a softy at heart. That was a moment that I will never forget.

After graduating from the academy each of us new officers had to work 10 weeks with a FTO (Field Training Officer). My first ten weeks were spent in the radio room where I was taught how to dispatch the calls on the police radio. The way FTO training works is that you work three weeks on first shift (A Platoon), three weeks on second shift (B Platoon) and three weeks on third shift (C Platoon). On the tenth week you go back to your initial starting shift and finish your ten week training. When I first learned that I was going to be in the FTO group to start in dispatch, I was very disappointed because I wanted to start in patrol. However, I realized I actually learned more about patrol and how calls were handled by working in dispatch, so I was grateful for the experience and for all that I had learned there.

When my ten weeks were over in dispatch, I continued on FTO in patrol for another ten weeks. The FTO training in patrol worked the same way with 3 weeks on each shift. I have to admit that my most interesting calls were on B Platoon (2nd shift). The officer that I was assigned to was also an old friend of my roommate, Patti, so we had something in common to break the ice. It just so happened that I experienced a few stabbings on the three weeks I spent on B Platoon. However, the most memorable one was a call we were dispatched to which was called in by a victim in one of the parks in the City. It was around 9:00 p.m. when we arrived at the scene. Upon arriving, we found a man in his early 20s lying on the ground with a stab wound in his left side. Lying on the ground next to the victim was a steak knife with the victim's blood on it. The victim stated that he had just asked his girlfriend to marry him and she turned him down. In his despair, he took a walk in the park near her home. He stated that while he was sitting on one of the benches sobbing, someone came up from behind him and tried to rob him. He claimed that he fought his attacker off before he was able to rob him, but sometime during the fight, he was stabbed.

My FTO officer called for an ambulance and we tended to the victim's wound. We asked the victim what the alleged attacker stole from him. The victim stated he his attacker was not able to steal anything because he was able to fight him off and get away. The victim emptied his pockets and showed us that he still had his wallet, cell phone and the engagement ring. When the ambulance arrived they rushed the victim to the hospital and we advised him that a detective would be visiting him at the hospital to take his statement. Before the ambulance left, my FTO told the victim that the knife would be turned in as evidence and would be checked for fingerprints. He further advised the victim that he better make sure that he didn't t lie in his statement to the detective, because if he does, he would be arrested for making a false statement.

When we got back to our cruiser, I asked my FTO why he made that remark about the statement to the victim. My FTO proceeded to tell me that he didn't believe a word of the victim's story about being attacked and stabbed, and that he was sure that the victim had stabbed himself. My training officer further stated that he had been on calls similar to this and was sure that the victim stabbed himself to get pity from his girlfriend. At first I was surprised that he had come to this conclusion about the stabbing, but the more I thought about it, it was sort of strange that nothing was stolen from the victim and the attacker left the knife with his fingerprints on it at the scene. Well, sure enough when we started our shift the next day, my FTO informed me that that the Detective Bureau notified him that our stab victim admitted to stabbing himself for attention from his girlfriend. Wow, nothing is ever as it appears!

When my ten week patrol FTO assignment was completed, I was assigned to B Platoon and began answering calls on my own. I was very grateful for all the training I received from my three FTOs and I felt that I was given lots of good advice and instruction to fall back on when I needed it. I really liked working patrol, the only difficult part is having to go into people's homes that were not very clean. The other unlikeable part of being on patrol was answering some of the nonsense complaints that the public calls the police for. Most people ask me all the time if I am scared to answer calls. Most calls are not dangerous calls, and when they are dangerous, the dispatcher will dispatch two or three patrol units to respond.

I began my patrol career on B Platoon (3:30 p.m. to 11:30 p.m.) That shift was very difficult for me because I never saw my family. At the time, all three children were teenagers. Our oldest just turned 16 and was anxious to get her license. Both our girls were cheerleaders at school and my husband had to bring them to practice every night and pick them up when they were done at 9:30 or so. My husband and family complained that they never saw me and it was getting to me too. After a year or so, I was able to go to C Platoon (11:30 to 7:30). The hardest part of working that shift was getting my sleep, but I was able to spend dinner time with my family and see the children when they go home from school.

One obstacle that I didn't think I would have had to overcome, was dealing with some of the mini-Rambos, as I called them. The mini-Rambos are the younger guys on the job who liked to try to belittle other officers on the job, especially the female officers. I maybe small in stature, but when one of these guys would try to pull their smart crap with me, I would put them in their place and remind them that I was old enough to be their mother and they better use a different tone when addressing me. Once I established my ground, things were good. However, at times the public would talk to me like that as well, and it would blow my mind how disrespectful people are.

The best part of my job is the opportunities to encourage people, to share God's love with them. I usually walked the beat downtown, but also worked on the road, in dispatch and the matron's office. I enjoyed my job and I always tried to make a difference, if I could. As a police officer we have the difficult job of trying to decide if a person or persons need to be arrested or given a summons, or if they should be given a warning. We do not have to arrest everyone that we are dealing with, however, we need to resolve the situation properly.

The most interesting part of my job are the people we meet and the homes we respond to. I was in a home interviewing complainants about something and out of the corner of my eye I notice something on the floor in the corner of the room. I completely lost my concentration on what the person was explaining to me and realized that it was a dead cat! I asked the woman is she had realized that her cat was dead and she told me that her brother was going to bury it later!!! What the hell??? There was a small child in the home at the time. After I completed my interview and resolved her matter, I instructed her to get a towel and bring the cat outside. She did as I asked her to and as I was walking back to my cruiser, I kept thinking that we just can't make this stuff up. The stories that we share with each other are entertaining to say the least!

Another great part of my job are the extra duty assignments. Extra duty jobs pay a flat rate of $50.00 hour and you are guaranteed four hours, even if your assignment ends in less than that. Extra duty assignments are jobs that we can take outside of our regular shift. Extra duty jobs could range from standing over a manhole while different utility companies do their work, working at the Mall or a local establishment to keep order or working a school gym for a basketball game. There was one extra duty job, however, that actually was the starting point for this book.

I received a call from the Extra Duty Office to see if I wanted to work this one particular Saturday. The Sergeant gave me a few jobs to choose from and then said there is "some kind of religious thing going on at the North End Recreation Center, some healing lady would you want that?" Well it was my lucky day. I can work extra duty and get to hear a message at the same time. A win-win for me.

I arrived at my assignment to find out that the religious event was Grace-N-Vessels, which I was very familiar with. This woman, Grace, and her team had a gospel and healing ministry. She would sing worship songs and she would also prophesy over the crowd. I was scheduled to arrive an hour before the actual meeting was to start to keep the crowd moving and keep any trouble makers out. While I was standing at the door the woman, Grace, came over to introduce herself to me and to thank me for working at her event. I told her that I was a Christian and that I had the opportunity to go to a couple of her events in the past. As we were talking, she asked me how I decided to become a police officer and I gave her a quick version of my story. She looked at me and said "God just showed me that He is going to use to you to touch many lives." I politely said "Thank you." She grabbed my hands and said "I'm serious. God wants you to write a book about your life and have it published and printed all over the country." I told her that I wouldn't even know where or how to begin to do that, but that I would definitely pray about it. She gave me a smile and a hug and said she would be waiting to read it someday.

During the service, I kept thinking about what she told me. I prayed, "God if this is really you, then you will have to guide me on this." A short time later a thought came in my mind loud and clear, the name of the book will be "Don't Tell Me I Can't".

CHAPTER 13

In the summer of 2008, there was a notice in our Police Bulletin that there was an opening at the Waterbury Police Activity League to run a Special Olympics program that was going to start in September. The Waterbury PAL, is a branch of the Waterbury Police Department that Chief Neil O'Leary reorganized after it was abandoned for years. A Sergeant and three or four officers were assigned to PAL at that time. The purpose of PAL was to bridge the gap between police officers and the children through sports and various activities. Now Special Olympics was being added to allow children with special needs an opportunity to participate in sports.

I applied for this position, along with three other officers. I was chosen for the position and I began working 9 to 5 at the PAL office in September of 2008. I was very nervous at first because I did not want to be considered a "secretary" because I already left that. I was advised that this position was an administrative position and that we still wore our badge and gun to work each day. It took me a few months to get into the routine at PAL, and I was also sent to get my bus driver's license. PAL had an old school bus donated to them that we at PAL had to learn to drive to transport children to various activities throughout the City and surrounding areas.

Also part of the contract between Special Olympics Connecticut and PAL was that an office had to be built at PAL specifically for the person who was chosen to run the Special Olympics program. So I also was given my own office at PAL. My family and friends were happy for me, especially since they felt that I was much safer at PAL than in patrol. The guys at PAL were all great and everyone got along and worked very well together. My heart was to work with children and I knew God had his hand in the decision.

I had not had much exposure to children with special needs up to this point. I was familiar with Eunice Kennedy Shriver and knew she had established Special Olympics for children and adults with special needs. Apparently, the President of Connecticut Special Olympics, Beau Doherty, was looking for an organization that served urban youth, in an effort to connect to the special needs children in urban areas, such as Waterbury. One of Connecticut Special Olympics largest sponsors, Mike Bozzuto, President of Bozzuto's, Inc., had suggested Mr. Doherty contact Waterbury PAL as a possible partnership opportunity. A meeting was held with the then Chief and President of Waterbury PAL, Neil O'Leary, and it was decided that Connecticut Special Olympics would have its first and only partnership with another nonprofit organization.

I also had the help of two of the Waterbury Special Olympics coaches, Nick and Rich, who helped me get familiar with all the Special Olympics forms and policies. Also, at this time Connecticut Special Olympics had just started their Unified Special Olympics Program. This unified program paired special needs athletes with partners, children without special needs, and had them compete in various sports to be more competitive and also to build friendships between the youth.

I started out at one of the Middle Schools and spoke with the various Special Ed Teachers and I was able to sign up a dozen or more athletes and partners and we began practicing volleyball in early October. Once I began to work with these youth on a regular basis, I began to have a new love and respect for these children.

With the help of Nick and Rich, I continued to the next sport, Track and Field, and I was able to sign up more and more athletes and partners. To date, PAL now has over 250 Special Olympics athletes and partners signed up with our PAL Special Olympics Program. We play year round, track and field in the spring, softball in the summer, volleyball in the fall and basketball in the winter. The joy and enthusiasm of the athletes is what keeps me going.

CHAPTER 14

DAYS TURNED INTO WEEKS, WEEKS turned into months and I never started my book, even though I knew that God wanted me to write it. I decided in December 2010, to purchase a laptop computer so that I could start typing my book anywhere, with no excuses. I started typing on a regular basis right away through the colder months, however, once the nice weather started to come around, I worked less and less on it. I had every excuse too, but none were really true. I was just simply too lazy and I had let the devil convince me that no one was going to read it anyways.

I brought my laptop on my first week vacation with my brother, Mike and his wife, Angel. We rented a house in Rhode Island for the week in July of 2011. I did work on the book during that week, but not diligently. I prayed God would understand that I needed to "relax and do nothing". I may have been a third of the way through at that point.

When I returned home from vacation, my husband had a new scooter waiting in the driveway for me. A few months prior I had mentioned to my husband that I was thinking of getting a scooter to go back and forth to work in, to save on gas, etc. Well here it was in my driveway, a bright red shiny scooter. On Sunday afternoon, my husband and son, got me on the scooter and showed me how to operate it. I started driving it on the grass around my house, but it was bumpy and I was struggling to ride it. I suggested that I would take it on the dead end road one house over. My husband and son were at the end of the driveway with me. That is the last thing that I remembered.

Next thing I know I woke up in the Emergency Room at the Hospital with my husband tell me that I hit a truck and that I broke my back, cracked my head open, tore off my nose and hurt myself pretty badly. I remember freaking out that I was paralyzed and he kept telling me to relax. My next memory is a week later being transported to a Rehabilitation Center.

Now I'm really freaking out. I'm in a convalescent home with all elderly people and I'm in a bed and can barely move. I guess my face was pretty bad too. Stitches in my forehead, black eyes, nose all stitched up. Arms all black, literally black, not black and blue. My family and friends told me that I was doing much better and I was starting to look more like myself. All I could think was that I would never be a cop again.

While I was in rehab I was told what exactly happened. I must have given the scooter too much gas as I was pulling out of my driveway and instead of turning right to go to the dead end street, I shot across the street and hit a Honda Pilot. Apparently, I tried to turn the scooter to avoid hitting the car, the scooter fell to the right and I fell to the left into path of the SUV. No damage to the scooter, but a small scratch on the brake handle. My poor husband and son saw the whole thing. I can't imagine the horror they must have felt.

So the nurses and staff explained my injuries to me. I had a large contusion on my head with 18 staples, I broke my left eye socket, ripped one side of my nose off, I had a compression fracture of my T5 vertebrae. I had a very large cut on my left elbow and cuts and bruises over most of my body. They assured me that I was going to recover, but I was really scared that I wasn't going to. After my first week in rehab, I was able to get out of bed into a wheelchair and was able to be showered. My hair was still full of blood and dirt. I could only see my arms and legs and all the bruises. I never saw what I looked like, and from what I heard, I'm probably glad I didn't. My family and friends visited me every day and I was never alone. My church family came and prayed for me. My work friends came to visit. Everyone was telling me how much better I was, but I never really knew how bad I was in the first place.

The day finally came that I would going to try to walk. I had to wear a metal turtle shell as soon as I got out of bed. The CNA brought me a walker!!! What the hell?? Please don't tell me that I'm going to need a walker. The aide assured me that it was for safety reasons until they felt that I could walk on my own. I walked up and down the hallway a few times, I felt like one of the elderly residents. The staff was cheering me on. I felt happy and sad at the same time.

Because of the contusion on my head, I was very nauseous. Every time I sat up the room would literally start spinning and I would vomit. I was taken back to the hospital for a MRI to make sure everything was all right. It was decided that I need some anti-nausea medicine, which finally helped after a few days.

Soon it was time for rehabilitation exercises. It was very slow to start, but I made progress. I was determined to get back to my old self. I felt as if I was trapped in my body. I asked God to give me the strength to do the exercises and to help me to BELIEVE that I was going to recover. I had my good days and bad days, but the staff was super encouraging, as well as my family and friends.

I was taken for doctor visits by ambulance to have my staples and stitches taken out. When I visited the doctor who stitched my nose he asked me if I remembered him from the hospital. I told him that I did not. He then told me that I probably didn't remember asking him to give me a Michael Jackson nose!! I told him that my husband told me that, but I thought he was kidding. The doctor told me that he was going to give me the nose I was born with.

I also was taken to the neurosurgeon who worked on my back. The doctor told me that I had a compression fracture of my T5. He compared my fracture to what a soda can looks like if you step on it. It was crushed. The brace was needed for my back to heal because there was no surgery to repair the damage. He took a lot of x-rays of my back and said that the injury looked the same as the day of my accident, which he said was a good thing. I wanted to ask him so badly if I would ever be a cop again, but I was too afraid of the answer.

After a month in rehab, I was told that I was going to be able to go home, but I was not able to leave the home without help. I had a physical therapist, a visiting nurse and an aide come to my home a few times a week to help me shower, check my wounds and do therapy. I was told this was going to be a slow recovery process. I returned home at the end of August. Now I had all the time I needed on my hands, no excuses, I worked on my book as much as I could. I wondered if God allowed this accident to slow me down enough to work on the book.

By November, the doctor allowed me to return to work. I couldn't drive so I had to get rides back and forth. I still had to continue to wear my back brace to work under my shirt and was only allowed to sit at my desk, answer the phones and take care of the people who came in to sign up their children. I was working "light duty" until the doctor cleared me for full duty. The final decision to return to full duty was up to the neurosurgeon. At this time, I still really didn't comprehend how serious my injuries were.

In December of 2011, I met with the neurosurgeon for my final ex-ray and evaluation. The doctor asked me if I felt I was ready to return to full duty. I told him that I felt I was ready. The nurse brought my final ex-rays in for the doctor to review. He tells me that my back is still the same. I told the doctor that I was disappointed because I prayed for God to give me a miracle and make my vertebrae grow back and the doctor looks me straight in the eye and tells me that I am a miracle!! The doctor explained to me that your spinal cord runs through the middle of your vertebrae and that I had compressed my vertebrae without damaging my spinal cord and that that is a miracle in itself. He then went on to explain to me that if the damaged vertebrae had moved at all and had not healed in place like it did, that I would have most likely been paralyzed from the waist down! Now I was beginning to understand why he would ask me at every visit if I was urinating myself or experiencing any numbness in my legs! Thank you Jesus for your protection was all that I could say.

The neurosurgeon then gave me written permission to return to full duty and told me that he is even more surprised than I was that he was actually allowing me to continue being a police officer and told me that I needed to slow down because I was in my early 50s and not a kid anymore. With that, we both stood up and hugged each other. I remember leaving his office feeling like I was given another chance at life and I knew God's hand was on me.

During the time of my rehabilitation, I struggled with the fact that I would not be able to return to full duty. I remember worrying that I would not regain my strength and mobility. In the beginning, I felt as if I was trapped inside of my own body. I hated having to depend on people to help me and I was upset that I had so many injuries. I was praying and talking to God one day and I asked Him why He could not have just moved the truck over a foot so that I wouldn't have gotten hurt. I heard the Lord speak to me that He did move the truck, that's why I was still alive!!! Wow, I never really looked at the accident that way. God was actually watching over me that day. Here I was alive and not paralyzed. Instead of complaining about everything, I knew that I had to start thanking the Lord for sparing my life and healing my body. Why did God spare my life? Did I have more work to do for Him? Could it be possible that my life would actually make a difference? God showed me that He has a purpose for my life. That I was here for a reason. I pray one of the reasons is that his book is going to make a difference in people's lives. That I can be of some encouragement, that no matter where you came from or what you've been through, that you can do whatever it is in your heart to do with your life. There are so many reasons why we can't do this or we can't do that. Many of those reasons come out of fear of failure or lack of encouragement to live your dreams.

Where are you today? Are you a young person who feels that no one cares about you? Are you a teenager that is struggling with peer pressure? Are you trying to figure out what career path you should go on? Are you a single mom trying to make ends meet? Are you a young/older man that always aspired to have that dream job? What is holding you back from trying to fulfil your dreams and goals?? God is no respecter of persons. He wants to bless us and provide all our needs. Don't you dare settle for less than God's best for your life. If you pray and ask God for direction for your life and trust Him, He will show you the best path to take. God will give you the confidence to accomplish anything that you set your mind to do. No one thought that a 47 year old, mother of three, would be able to become a police officer. I prayed and asked God for a job where I could be a light in this world. I prayed for a job somewhere in the legal field. I did some research on what qualifications were necessary to become a police officer and I knew that I had the legal knowledge to pass a written exam, but I needed to start exercising and getting in better shape to qualify for the physical aspect. I prayed and asked God that if it was His will for me to become a police officer then I was going to trust Him to open the doors. I prayed that if the doors were shut, then I would consider another field. God kept opening doors. I passed a few written tests in other departments and passed the physical tests as well. However, I was not getting any job offers. Since I kept getting very close, I knew God was still opening doors for me and that eventually He was going to open the right one for me. I didn't listen to others when they tried to tell me that I should stop trying to become a police officer. I had to stay focused and believe that God would open the right door at the right time. If I had listened to those who told me that I was too old, too short or that the job was too difficult for me, I wouldn't be where I am today. But I stood in faith and believed God and He did open the doors for me.

The purpose of this book is to encourage people from all walks of life. Trust me, just look at the media, money does not buy you happiness. Please don't let money be your goal. I know we all need money to survive and raise a family, but get your priorities in order. Don't let your past keep you from your future. Start today to make the changes necessary to live your life and achieve your goals. Remember, don't let anyone tell you 'YOU CAN'T".

CPSIA information can be obtained
at www.ICGtesting.com
Printed in the USA
BVOW06s1920130417

481226BV00009B/309/P

9 781530 707775